I0558105

Stuttering

Learn to Control Your Stuttering by Beating the Anxiety

(Making for Parents and Professionals Who Love and Teach Kids Who Stutter)

Perry Weymouth

Published By **Bella Frost**

Perry Weymouth

Stuttering: Learn to Control Your Stuttering by Beating the Anxiety (Making for Parents and Professionals Who Love and Teach Kids Who Stutter)

ISBN 978-1-998038-73-2

Legal & Disclaimer

Upon using the information contained in this book, you agree to hold harmless the Author from and against any damages, costs, and expenses, including any legal fees potentially resulting from the application of any of the information provided by this guide. This disclaimer applies to any damages or injury caused by the use and application, whether directly or indirectly, of any advice or information presented, whether for breach of contract, tort, negligence, personal injury, criminal intent, or under any other cause of action.

You agree to accept all risks of using the information presented inside this book. You need to consult a professional medical practitioner in order to ensure you are both able and healthy enough to participate in this program.

Table Of Contents

Chapter 1: Why We Stutter

•More men stutter than girls.

This is interesting. There's loads of stuttering Stanleys however not many stuttering Stacys. Are there persona dispositions that men have that purpose them to much more likely to stutter?

•Stuttering develops in humans, but it isn't always placed out.

You aren't born with it, but it takes place sincerely.

•About five% of the region develops a short stutter as a infant. About 1% maintain it for life.

There's no regulation saying which you need to be stuck with it.

•People who stutter regularly have intervals in which the stutter receives better however then comes lower back. This is normal.

There may be environmental motives on your lifestyles that make you stutter.

•People who stutter frequently try to rush through a sentence out of fear they'll stutter. This frequently seems to make the stutter worse.

You're strolling faraway from the verbal exchange due to the reality you're terrified of talking. But, are you afraid due to the reality you stutter, or do you stutter due to the truth you're afraid?

•Stutterers generally try to avoid conversations.

At one element, I notion I avoided conversations because of my stutter. Now I accept as authentic with my avoidance and my stutter percentage a common motive.

•The severity of the stutter can range throughout top notch conditions.

Again, the surroundings or placing seems to be a component.

I bet that during case you stutter like me, you examine the above statistics with a few degree of astonishment at how appropriately they defined you. It's like analyzing the zodiac description of your personality. Depending on how lengthy you've had a stutter, you can pair those information together collectively along with your non-public experience to collect the puzzle portions and in reality understand your stuttering.

This permits us to get beyond some of the inaccurate tries to accurate a stutter. For example, you can had been advised to talk slowly to reduce your stutter. I become knowledgeable this throughout speech remedy as a little one. It's logical to hypothesize that stuttering is a clean fumbling of terms due to speaking too rapid, in which the mind has a sort of glitch inside the "make the mouth glide" quarter. So, the herbal answer is to slow down. However, this speculation appears to be incorrect. But at the same time as the solution of slowing down is surely on the right song, it desires to be described a piece better. We'll look closer at that in Capter 2: How to Stop Stuttering.

To advantage a deeper records into why I stutter, I first had to investigate the conditions wherein I generally generally tend to have trouble talking, which include while:

•Meeting new people.

•Speaking to customers at artwork.

•Speaking inside the the the front of a crowd.

•Giving terrible facts or telling someone a few difficulty that I expect they don't need to pay interest.

•Sensing or believing the opportunity individual is irritated with me.

•Expecting to be admonished.

This is typically while you're a baby stepping into hassle, but the fear can subconsciously live with you in adulthood.

•Fearing a horrible final effects after speakme.

When I look at this listing, I see a not unusual trait—one which's absent during instances as quickly as I wouldn't stutter. Most of the conditions in which I don't have any hassle speaking are whilst:

•I'm irritated.

The humorous factor is, if I'm stuttering and the listener gives me any trace of ridicule about it, I get a touch irritated, and the stutter is going away.

•I'm studying aloud or reciting a few aspect, along with lyrics or a short speech.

•I'm on my own and questioning out loud.

I sincerely have in reality no problem talking as soon as I'm by myself.

•I'm supporting a person in want.

•I'm captivated with what I'm saying or giving someone accurate information that I assume will cause them to glad.

•Someone makes me laugh and I reply.

•I'm speaking to very near buddies or family.

•I'm underneath the influence of alcohol or every distinct substance that relaxes me or elevates my mood.

Comparing the 2 lists, the maximum obvious scenario take into account is the presence or absence of tension. This seems to be the difficulty in a communique that determines if I will stutter or not. You might also moreover see specific elements of this. You can also additionally see it as fear or loss of self notion, however it all comes all the way down to my degree of anxiety approximately the communication. You may be questioning, "Well that's quite common. Lots of mother and father stutter a bit once they get involved, however I stutter all the time." You are correct. You and I stutter all of the time. That's the difference amongst us and every person else—we're nearly constantly as a minimum a bit annoying about speakme to human beings, and our anxiety manifests as a stutter.

You see, that is the reason for every my stutter and my quiet, introverted demeanor at social gatherings. I truly have social anxiety that stems from a thirst for approval: I want every body to like me. That's why I need to make humans giggle. That's why I want to visit social gatherings. I want humans to love me, however I'm afraid they acquired't. I'm afraid that when I open my mouth, I'll seem like an fool. So, my stutter isn't in reality a speech problem. At its root, it is an tension and vanity problem. And you're likely the equal way. I'll guess that whilst you are for your way to satisfy new human beings, you high-quality recall whether or not or not or no longer or no longer they'll collectively with you. You possibly don't even recall which you can now not like a number of them. It's a for the reason that you may find they all to be wonderful. In your thoughts, you are the handiest one human beings may not like.

Now, the motive of my stutter can range a tiny bit, counting on the situation. For instance, at paintings I might stutter because of the truth I understand there are likely terrible effects if I say topics my bosses or clients don't like. I certify cleanrooms and unique clean air devices, typically in the clinical region, and feature ordinary performance tension due to the immoderate stakes. Clients depend on me to live compliant with their guidelines, which means that that I should cause them pretty a few grief if I don't have proper information for them or don't do my task properly. People don't continuously react kindly at the same time as you ruin their day, that would cause terrible matters for me. So, stuttering at paintings is frequently out of a fear of failure as a expert.

When I stutter with buddies and circle of relatives at social gatherings, but, it's typically because of what I name "movie superstar goggles." When I'm searching for approval from humans in my social life, it stems from seeing all of us as being, via hook or through crook, above me. In my mind, they may be all either smarter, cooler, or greater successful than me. To paraphrase a line from the film The forty-Year-Old Virgin, I located them on a pedestal. I've even observed that when I consider humans I apprehend, I often cause them to taller in my creativeness than they will be in real existence. When I see them in character, I assume, "Have they normally been that brief?" Even if the man or woman is an inch or two shorter than me, I undergo in mind myself without a doubt looking as much as them. My thirst for their approval will increase the stakes of the conversation.

So, whether or now not it's for paintings or satisfaction, my speech impediment is prompted thru a want for approval. Anxiety approximately the approval reasons an epinephrine response in my thoughts. Most people have heard of the "fight or flight reaction," it's far at the same time as you both get competitive to fend off threat or run away to maintain yourself. This is because of epinephrine, a neurotransmitter in the thoughts. What plenty of human beings don't apprehend, despite the fact that, is that there's certainly a 3rd alternative: "fight, flight, or freeze." You might also come to be the proverbial "deer within the headlights" whilst hazard is spherical. If you're a stutterer, this might be the case with you. Your instinct is to not make a flow into or sound and wish you slip thru omitted.

This is exactly what stuttering is. When you attempt to speak, your thoughts instinctively says, "NO! DON'T DRAW ANY ATTENTION TO YOURSELF! DON'T MAKE A

SOUND AND THEY WON'T NOTICE YOU!" Your brain will reduce off the feed of terms on your mouth so at the same time as you try to flow your lips, no sound comes out. You just have an terrific feeling for your throat like the terms are being physical blocked there, almost like a localized paralysis. It's the same reason you could't suppose of things to say to join in the conversation. Your mind is hiding within the corner till it feels you're out of the woods. Your brain needs you to move omitted so that you don't get the terrible give up end result you fear. That worry is form of usually irrational and unfounded, however your herbal instincts, which best act in phrases of existence or loss of life, have a "better steady than sorry" attitude.

Conversely, as soon as I speak fluently, I'm either round people with whom I'm very comfortable or over whom I honestly have some form of perceived authority. This may be my spouse, daughter, longtime friends, very near family humans, a person beneath me at work, or someone who's quite more younger. If I experience that I already have the approval I are in search of for and might't lose it, or if I haven't any doubt in what I'm saying and might't see any capacity poor final results, then the pressure is off, and I received't stutter the least bit.

When at artwork, speaking fluently is also helped via way of using being an professional at the problem handy. I locate that once I'm assured inside the difficulty rely, I each gained't stutter, or it's going to not often be widespread. It will regularly look like I clearly favored a 1/2-second to keep in mind the proper word. This can be very just like stuttering however without the stammered syllables or the pressure. When talking to clients at art work, if I can see myself as helping or teaching them,

I'm an awful lot a bargain much less possibly to stutter. This is as it's a great deal much less hard to assume a herbal function of authority whilst giving useful aid. You enjoy like a piece hero, triggering a serotonin reaction within the mind, and the tension is going away. This moreover can be utilized in diverse social situations, which includes at the identical time as giving pointers, instructions, or explaining some factor to a pal.

The huge takeaway from this financial ruin is that your stutter is not truly a speech problem. It's a conceitedness problem. This is why loads of the conventional recommendation like "slow down" isn't effective. Speech treatment can often be an exercising in treating handiest the symptom of the trouble, due to the truth that's what stuttering is. It's the part of the trouble that you hate the maximum, however you can't alternate it with out addressing the vanity problem at its root. Like the Russian mobster inside the movie The Dark Knight said, "The clown turn out to be proper. We need to restore actual problem."

Chapter 2: How to Stop Stuttering

In this chapter, we'll pass over each brief brief-time period fixes to make your stutter milder and prolonged-term fixes to restriction your stutter so it's not a chronic supply of embarrassment.

Raise Your Self-Esteem

We'll begin with the lengthy-term solution: raising your vanity. This is the large one. You can't restore your stutter without correcting this problem, and sadly, it's lots less complicated stated than completed. But, fear no longer. I'll inform you the call of the game I've discovered for enhancing my self-esteem. You see, the term "shallowness" is a misnomer. The trouble isn't that you suppose too lowly of yourself, it's which you fail to apprehend that everybody else sucks just as lots as you do.

You've heard the phrase "no person is fine," right? Well, because the saying goes, anybody can be very an prolonged manner from high-quality—like "couldn't see excellent with the Hubble telescope" far— and they all are aware of it. It's a reality: even the celebrities you can appearance as much as on TV and in one in all a type media make each day mistakes, and that they have completed topics they remorse. A lot of them aren't even the humans you decided they may be. That's why people say you need to in no way meet your heroes. We have a natural tendency to idolize humans. But the fact is that none of these humans are honestly any better than you. They may additionally moreover moreover have decided on a profession course that made them famous, but that doesn't reason them to excellent, or even constantly correct human beings. And you can follow this to all of us for your lifestyles.

I'm reminded of a Bible verse from the Book of Matthew, chapter 19. You likely recognize the part approximately the rich man and the camel passing through the attention of the needle. Everyone makes a speciality of that segment, however there's something Jesus says proper earlier than that, which is probably the maximum disregarded passage of the New Testament. The wealthy man refers to Jesus as "Good Teacher." Before Jesus answers the wealthy man's query, he asks, "Why do you call me top? No one is proper but God." Jesus modified into absolutely along with himself even as he stated nobody is proper. It's a profound assertion that teaches us that all of us must conflict every day to make ourselves higher, lest our natural tendency to do awful will pop out. We additionally must resist the tendency to adore others. While it's precise to see the good trends in surely every body, this may come to be risky if taken too an extended manner. If that occurs then you definately definately discover yourself studying this ebook to discover ways to forestall stuttering; you've given yourself a complicated. But on the first rate facet, if you ever sense like a b-hollow after a lapse in judgement, take solace, due to the fact you're quite much like Jesus, bro ;).

Don't assume I'm telling you to be suggest or disrespectful to human beings. I'm simply telling you to take off the celebrity goggles while you view others. Instead of seeing a person as better than you, try seeing yourself in them, because we're all pretty masses the same. When you could see yourself in others, it makes you experience greater comfortable with them. You'll be more open and comfortable.

Once you are starting up the movie superstar goggles and begin seeing greater of yourself in others, you realize they're searching out approval too. It certainly doesn't have an effect on them the same manner it influences you. On the floor, they will appear assured, but everyone has instances once they're secretly as stressful as a Branch Davidian at an ATF office. (Did you get the reference? I suggested you about my humor.)

Some people say they don't care what others remember them, however this isn't absolutely correct. They can be properly enough with someone getting angry with them, but each person positioned at the least some of our self-worth in what our pals think about us. Everyone requires a few degree of approval. The ones who without a doubt don't are installed unique centers wherein they're not allowed to head away. We call the ones human beings sociopaths. We are social beings. It's our interactions and collaborations with different humans which have allowed us to make such terrific achievements in society. It's what lets in us to have a society the least bit. It's due to this that your worry of dropping approval is instinctual. It's a survival mechanism, and now not a totally conscious choice. That's why it's tough to trade. It takes time and effort to recondition your self, but every body can do it, and solving your self-esteem is the critical foundation. Remember to see yourself in others. Recognizing that they percentage the identical fears and aspirations of fulfillment is fundamental. And ultimately, making others plenty much less threatening will do wonders to your talking capability.

Build Your Confidence

There are self assure-building sports you may soak up to assist mitigate the demanding epinephrine reaction you get whilst speakme to people. Having self guarantee in your self and in what you're saying goes an prolonged way to stopping the stutter in advance than it begins.

As I noted in advance, having self guarantee in what I say goes an extended manner at art work. Taking pleasure to your artwork, being diligent in gaining knowledge of your interest to and fro offers you the self belief to claim what you're saying. Ergo, you're a outstanding deal much less probable to stutter. Be conscious that this also takes some trial and mistakes. Sometimes you're going to slip up and be wrong. This is a excellent time to do not forget that everyone else does too. Don't permit yourself start wondering too pretty of others even as you've made a mistake.

One of the quality methods to collect your personal self guarantee is with opposition. Through my stint as an novice MMA fighter, I determined out to mitigate worry and nerves. I noticed how the body's everyday typical overall performance suffers from them, which includes thru loss of a few manipulate over number one motor talents or perhaps clean selection-making. I needed to discover ways to not psych myself out earlier than a fight.

The nice advice I had been given, which I notwithstanding the truth that look at to situations in my normal existence, emerge as to not assume earlier to the upcoming feared disaster. I had to keep from thinking such things as, "I'll get punched within the face," "I'll get choked," "I'll get knocked out," "I'll lose in the front of everybody." It's useless to stay on consequences that haven't came about however. Instead, take the entirety one step at a time. Think, "I'm actually getting warmed up," "I'm really getting my fingers taped," "I'm definitely taking walks out,"

"We're virtually touching gloves," "I'm without a doubt doing my footwork, throwing a jab here, a hook there, subjects I've finished one million and one instances." In special terms, preserve a "we'll skip that bridge whilst we come to it" mind-set. Breaking the entirety down into portions makes large responsibilities viable, and keeps you centered in the 2d. Control what you may manipulate, and react to the topics as they upward thrust up. You'll find out they may be never as awful as you feared, and you're flawlessly capable of managing them.

Just taking on a full-touch martial art (which encompass grappling sports activities activities sports like Jiu-Jitsu) does wonders to help you mitigate strain. When you get beat up some instances steady with week, you discover that human beings being indignant with you outside the health club is not a huge deal. I suggest taking over some form of competitive game to construct your self belief and assist you learn how to deal with your nerves. And even if you don't compete, you continue to get severa advantage.

Practice Speaking to People

This one is easy in theory, but it is able to be the toughest to do. As masses as you cannot love it, you want to take the possibility to speak to people as often as feasible. Try to make your self carry on a conversation with a person. Part of learning is getting enough enjoy with it so that it will understand it. There may be an entire lot of trial and blunders, however you'll studies firsthand that human beings gained't react negatively to what you've got were given to mention. Practicing this over time will permit you to get better at thinking of things to mention. You'll additionally discover ways to be given that people will disagree with you every now and then, and that it's no longer the surrender of the arena. You could probably even get into a little debate, and that's really exceptional. Just be respectful, and also you'll see that topics will stay tame. You may additionally worry that no character wants to hear what you have to say, but you'll locate that most conversations don't need to be very interesting. You don't want to wow them. People typically truly need to fill the gap and spot that different human beings relate with them. It doesn't take a lot.

Chapter 3: Quick Fixes for Your Stutter

1.   Talk collectively along with your palms. This is a notable hack that works wonders for retaining me from getting caught on a word. When I revel in myself beginning to stutter, I discover that using hand gestures to go along with my phrases maintains my mind centered on what I'm saying and permits me to form of power through the stutter. When you stutter, your mind is walking far from the state of affairs. Somehow, getting your arms worried for your speech forces your mind again into the communique.

Hand gestures moreover help you installation and preserve a rhythm to your speech, which helps the phrases go along with the flow. Think of it in conjunction with you're the conductor of your private choir. I locate that slightly exaggerated gestures art work better, however you don't need to get loopy. It's outstanding to get into the dependancy of doing this from the start. Make it a ordinary a part of your mannerisms. The beauty of this is it's so easy to do however it gives you this shape of powerful and immediately advantage. That's why I listed this one first. You can begin doing this the very next time you communicate, and also you'll be quite pleased with the quit end result.

2.   Speak lightly, not slowly. When the speech therapist recommended me to slow down, she come to be at the right tune, but as I've explained, the trouble is which you get too traumatic. You need to learn to calm your self down, and this may take pretty a few workout. Taking up a self notion-building interest will assist. Keeping calm is the essential component. It takes a honest quantity of exercise that allows you to calm yourself down immediately, however you'll get it after a while. The subsequent four hints deliver a similarly

breakdown of preserving calm that will help you determine out a way to do it, but it's a few thing you could wonderful genuinely have a study thru experience.

three.　　Take on a function or character. I'm not telling you to be a person you're not. Let's get that immediately. I'm using the opposite of the recommendation where I told you to appearance your self in others. Start seeing others in yourself. Think of a person you want to observe or listen to, and try to make their style of talking a part of yours. You could possibly need to emulate a person who speaks with a non violent demeanor, like Matthew McConaughey (Ben Shapiro is for advanced college university college students). This works due to the fact you trick your mind into feeling such as you're projecting someone else in area of your self, which makes you sense an awful lot much less uncovered. Everyone does this to a degree. You in all likelihood speak masses like actually one in all your dad and mom or your remarkable pal. We look at nearly the whole lot we do from looking other humans and copying them.

2.   Stop rehearsing what you want to mention in advance of time. This normally applies to cellular phone conversations. Contrary to reciting a few component you've memorized, rehearsing what you want to mention right earlier than a cellular phone call will now not assist you. When you're doing this, what you're absolutely doing is attending to the forestall of the communication to your mind. This is each other manner to run from the opportunity to talk. You're definitely wishing you have got been already executed with the trade. Focus on the instant, and take it little by little. (No "That's what he said" jokes!)

three.　　Pause and breathe. When you begin to stutter, take a half-second pause and a short breath. That can be simply sufficient time to refocus on what you're pronouncing, and a short pause is lots higher than stammering on a word.

four.　　Accept that you're having a conversation. Remember to take subjects one step at a time. This applies for your speech as well. Focus on what you're pronouncing right now. Don't anticipate ahead to what they may say or what you can say to what they'll say again. Immerse your self in the communique and don't rush. Stay calm. Rushing is some different way to run some distance out of your tension. Keep calm and communicate on.

5.　　Look the opposite character in the attention. This will work wonders for calming down a verbal exchange, and it's an instantaneous boom in your self warranty. It is available in specially available on the identical time as a few jerk is getting an thoughts-set with you. When a person is providing you with crap, get up directly with rectangular shoulders and stare them right away in the attention with a smooth expression for your face. They will without delay look away and their tone will melt. You've tapped into their subconscious and tricked them into wondering, "This man is not any beta." It's an instinctual problem. They understand they may instead now not have a fight. They should be honestly mad at you for this not to art work, however if that's the case, you're probably virtually as mad at them. I noticed a truly right (albeit creepy) instance of this in a YouTube video in which the suspect, a nerdy thin extra younger man, used this bypass at the "bad cop" detective for the duration of an interrogation. I found this method prolonged in advance than seeing this video, however this video is a extremely good instance of strategies powerful it may be. If you need to have a have a look at it, the video is known as "The Bizarre Case of Stephen McDaniel" at the YouTube channel JCS - Criminal Psychology. I don't propose using the creepy voice he uses although.

6.	Start each verbal exchange with a type greeting. Using this trick does topics. One, it makes the alternative individual reciprocate your kindness which brings down everyone's pressure. And , having a desired starting to a verbal exchange acts as a cue to get you in the swing of factors so that you can communicate greater fluently.

I use the ones 8 hacks in my every day lifestyles to assist me communicate with little to no stuttering. I'm confident my little tricks of the alternate will are to be had available for you too. Again, it'd, of direction, take a piece practice, however don't get discouraged. This is like maximum subjects in existence, in that as long as you accept as true with you may do it, then you could do it. Mindset is everything.

Chapter 4: The Deposition

As promised within the advent, right right here comes the more ominous tale. Back in 2013, I were given in a car twist of destiny whilst my work van hit a patch of ice at the interstate. My van spun round 100 and eighty levels and I modified into hit head-on via an 18-wheeler. Luckily, I changed into now not injured. Everyone turn out to be going gradual sufficient that the collision most effective hammered the the front-surrender of my van and now not me.

About years later, I were given a call from my boss saying the organisation end up being sued over that twist of destiny, and I even have turn out to be named as a co-defendant. I had quite a few explaining to do as a protracted way as filling in our attorneys, and if you want to speak about anxiety… Son, permit me inform you.

As expected, things got worse earlier than they have been given better. For folks who don't comprehend, in case you're concerned in a jail suit, a deposition is if you have to are available and answer questions from the opposing legal professional. So, it's a veiled term for an interrogation. In the case of a civil wholesome over private harm, stated legal professional will want to bombard you with inquiries to get you to unwittingly incriminate yourself so that you can use it inside the route of you in courtroom docket; it's their manner to find out a way to use your very personal terms in opposition to you.

The night time time before my deposition, I drove as much as our jail professional's workplace so he may also want to put together me for the onslaught earlier. (The case happened approximately 3 hours from wherein I stay thinking about I became journeying out of city while the twist of fate came about.) Part of it end up filling me in on procedural stuff. He went over the collection for the way the questions cross: opposing lawyer asks a query, my felony professional gadgets, then I can answer the query.

But then, he had been given to the critical element that calls for the actual prep paintings. He began out telling me about what they in the enterprise call "reptile questions." These are just like "gotcha questions" in journalism. These are sly traps designed to make you appearance responsible or to discredit you. They are indistinct questions on substantial morality or duty. They can be disguised as seemingly aim truths like, "Do you believe you studied protection on the road is your primary duty?" wherein your answer can incriminate you after the opposing felony professional receives into specifics of the case wherein they use this as a framing tool to show which you had been irresponsible. Alternatively, they'll be overly subjective questions imagined to make you speculate, that may be a terrible concept in a courtroom due to the fact hypothesis is assumption, and you apprehend what takes region whilst you ass/u/me. If you answer wrong, you've truly handed the opposing council a club with which to overcome you over the pinnacle at trial.

The simplest viable way out is to channel your internal Bill Clinton and live away from, live faraway from, keep away from. You must offer you along with your very own sly tactic to answer the questions with out virtually answering the questions. You have to refute the idea of the query itself and supply an reason behind why the query is bunk for the jury's (in this situation the destiny jury's) sake. This isn't always any stroll inside the park for every body, but for someone whose terms can near down in worrying situations round strangers, permit's just say subjects had been not looking up.

To get through this ordeal, I had to use every approach I knew. Every tip I listed earlier emerge as hired, and I had to have conquered my self guarantee and shallowness troubles. Basically, I had been given via the deposition much like I got thru every MMA combat—one little step at a time. I didn't allow myself see the opposing criminal expert as a danger who grow to be equipped to consume my lunch. I didn't assume ahead to the reputedly inevitable hammer that emerge as coming down any 2d for a wrong solution. When he walked within the room, I greeted him with a grin and a type salutation. He reciprocated and took his seat right now throughout from me, with my attorney to my left. I sat in advance in my chair, barely leaned over the table. The stenographer sat down and installation her machine, and we had been given began.

The starting of the deposition modified into not whatever unique. To get every body on the identical web web page, the opposing attorney started with a few procedural questions to get primary statistics, i.E., my call and wherein I stay, how lengthy I'd been at my interest.

Then, he started out in search of to make some small talk, for loss of a better term. At least, that's the way it's supposed to appearance. He asked me approximately subjects I did at my task, which had now not some thing right now to do with the twist of future. Part of this became simply to appearance if I'd supply him a few trouble he ought to use in opposition to me or the enterprise employer, and maximum people should no longer assume to find out such subjects from these "small speak" questions. He become looking for something that made the employer appearance negligent. And due to the truth the questions went on, his cause have turn out to be extra apparent.

The distinct purpose he started out out with the less complicated questions changed into to try to soften me up. The concept turned into if he may additionally need to make me get fine with him, I'd expose extra facts that he might also need to apply in opposition to me, making his undertaking a good deal less complex. He desired me to step on a land mine.

This a part of the deposition genuinely got here natural to me. My tendency to be shy and give short answers served me well. The largest difficulty to take into account at the same time as being deposed isn't to offer answers to questions that weren't asked. Make them pry the data out of you, and within the occasion that they bypass over a few issue, oh well. The principal distinction most of the deposition and the manner I generally behave is I desired to mission a certain quantity of strength. I idea if I got here for the duration of as timid, it'd encourage him to emerge as extra competitive along together with his questions. The difficult component at some stage in this section of the deposition became balancing my attitude among seeing the opposing prison professional as someone who's no longer a danger so I won't get intimidated but additionally maintaining in thoughts that he's not my buddy, and he's now not there to help me.

I stuttered instances sooner or later of those questions. (The stenographer have become great enough to put in writing them into the transcript.) They were mild, but I knew I had to recompose myself. I took a breath and modified my mind-set from being an excessive amount of on the aspect of preventing for my life to one which's closer to surely answering easy questions. I had to remind myself that whilst the guy asking me the questions supposed me some harm, it's not a few issue I couldn't manipulate. He's a person similar to me. I remembered the advice my crook professional gave me in advance than, and I trusted in his guidance.

The subsequent part of the thinking is wherein I needed to provide you with a few slightly clever answers. These are the "reptile questions" wherein in case you bought his premise and deliver a clean answer, you're wrong because of the reality the concept of his query is that you're accountable. This modified into the maximum hard issue because of the fact I knew that if I started out stuttering, it is probably seen as a chink in my armor, a vulnerability, and that might deliver gasoline to the hearth. It might possibly even appear like I'm mendacity.

He threw the primary one at me. After verifying I have been given a rate price price ticket for careless driving, he requested if I felt I deserved the price charge tag. Even reading the transcript now, six years later, it strikes a nerve. My treatment for preserving my composure have end up being examined. The opposing lawyer desired to try to enhance a piece emotion in me so I might likely try and protect myself. He knew I might both get stuck in a lie or look like a terrible individual who avoids taking obligation. That meant sticking to the game plan grow to be more crucial than ever. But I slipped a touch and spoke back no. I hadn't determined out this became one of the gotcha questions until my legal expert objected, however I'd already all began out my solution. I said I felt the damaging avenue conditions have been the motive of the accident (at the peak of the ice fall, there was about four inches at the floor). Now I knew the gauntlet became down. Game on.

In the very subsequent question, the opposing legal expert requested me to apportion a percentage of blame a number of the 3 drivers involved within the accident. For a piece greater heritage information, the truck that hit me moreover sideswiped a passing truck at the equal time as swerving to try and avoid me. In one in every of a kind terms, this man favored me to have the trial inside the direction of myself right then and there in my head, and he desired me to tell him how accountable I became. Here modified into my answer:

Chapter 5: That's a very tough question to reply

situation with the weather gambling this type of large function. I

anticipate it simply is virtually -- however I ought to have to say it in reality is why

we have trials, due to such things as that."

I credit score rating my legal professional for making geared up me for a question like this. The surrender of my solution is pretty a bargain verbatim from what he knowledgeable me the night time time earlier than. (Thank God for insurance to pay for exact attorneys.) I didn't stutter in my solution at all; the damage in the textual content is wherein I redirected my answer after remembering my attorney's advice. I took my time with my phrases, speakme frivolously. I didn't allow my mind run away. I immersed myself in the communication. I embraced it, appeared him in the attention and brought my response, come what may additionally.

The felony expert right away asked extra follow-up reptile questions. He favored me to say if I concept each of the opposite drivers have been performing some issue wrong. He preferred me to both admit guilt or look terrible with the beneficial aid of blaming others.

I counseled him I couldn't provide him an answer due to the reality I surely didn't recognise what the opportunity drivers were doing. I wasn't going to make investments. I didn't stutter via any of these answers. In truth, my responses came out so fast that my horrible prison expert barely had time to item to the questions. I end up 3 or 4 phrases in in advance than he become capable to speak up.

I bet I surpassed the test of letting the opposing legal expert apprehend I wasn't going to incriminate myself, due to the reality the questions have been given more dull and well-known after that. He actually requested who I spoke to, if all people took photos, such things as that. He desired to comprehend if there have been witnesses to interview.

When springing up with my solutions, I pretended every query have grow to be the very last one, inside the feel that I didn't permit myself worry approximately how long this will maintain. Once I had been given going, I nearly welcomed the project. This is the kind of mind-set you need to defeat your stutter, however you may't do it without addressing your shallowness. I didn't image the attorney throwing an answer lower back in my face. I didn't worry the least bit about what he became going to do. I truly believed that I can be able to manipulate something he threw at me.

The entire technique lasted multiple hours, and I didn't have any hassle growing with responses to the questions. The few times I did stutter, it changed into slight, and some of them may also need to with out problems have been perceived as a easy pause to bear in mind a word. In trendy, I stuttered seven instances. Four of them may be happened as a easy pause or a everyday repeat. In one sentence, I said, "...in-in-within the metropolis." Another time I stated, "It-it-it...I want to say it did it as a minimum 4 instances." And one final time I stated, "It-it-it's the equal version." Those were my 3 stammers that I couldn't cowl. All-in-all, I'm very happy with how fluid I modified into.

Afterwards, I requested my jail expert how I did. He informed me I did properly, and he wouldn't change any of my answers. He stated how I end up beforehand and engaged the complete time. Body language can't be neglected right right here. We speak just as masses with our posture and gestures as we do with our phrases. Body language is a critical detail to fixing the stutter equation.

So, you can see I used each trick in the e-book:

•I didn't allow myself hype up the lawyer I modified into speakme to. Instead, I noticed myself in him and noticed that he have become just a guy like me.

•I had self belief in myself knowledge that I have turn out to be certainly capable of succeeding at this.

•I took the whole thing one step at a time, not residing on what might be to return.

•I common that there is probably some confrontational speakme, and I stored it calm and well mannered (and the prison expert reciprocated).

•I took my time with my solutions. I made my thoughts reputation on what I become pronouncing in desire to skipping to the cease of the sentence in which I didn't have to speak anymore.

•I used body language, in this case, to every project strength and self belief and to keep my thoughts targeted while installing a rhythm to my speech.

The plaintiff ended up settling out of court docket docket, accepting the coverage organisation's provide, as is form of commonly the case, and now not some thing too lousy came out of it. I ended up a chunk wiser than I end up earlier than, from both the damage and the healthful. If I can get through some element like this, having to conquer my stutter, then there's no real reason you can't overcome yours.

Chapter 6: A Child's Speech

Idreaded paying attention to my call known as in magnificence, pleasant to be left reputation susceptible and exposed. The mere concept of it brought me lots worry and tension.

I hated the feeling that I constantly had been given inside the pit of my belly after I had to mention a few thing out loud in front of a hard and fast of humans, mainly at the same time as my terms were unplanned and unrehearsed. Rather than the combat or flight reaction that a few humans get, the concern itself rendered me frozen and foggy.

I modified into unable to accumulate my mind or piece together what I preferred to say. I stood by myself feeling humiliated with out everybody to rescue me or help string collectively the unraveling thoughts and terms indoors of my head. I have emerge as rendered speechless with only a cascading mess of umms and uhhs to shuffle via. The highbrow replay of stumbling over my terms nearly jolted me right right into a panic assault.

Mostly, I hated not being capable of percent freely, the one issue that I needed I should have manipulate over at the identical time because it mattered most--- my phrases.

They have to assume I'm slow or incapable of status as lots because the task, or worse, they should assume I'm a fraud. Sure, my grades were awesome; in reality, I never saw my first 'C' till once I'd graduated from immoderate college with honors, however what right are superior grades without a strong voice to lower again them. "What top is it to be inside the top 10% of your elegance if you cannot even deliver a easy speech?" modified into the concept that often flooded my head. I'd reasoned that I couldn't surely be remarkable on paper and failure within the the front of all of us. Honestly, it changed into a mortifying feeling that I can although experience the sting of once I permit my thoughts to move again to the ones dreadful instances. Times where I felt like my voice changed into simply being choked out of me thru fear. Times of trembling and sweating through splendor shows, however usually, instances of feeling like a defeated failure.

Instead of compassion and information, I were given the familiar look of pity. I should constantly see it in their eyes, at least in the ones that stayed spherical lengthy sufficient to look at me fumble over my damaged phrases. It should normally start as a rhythmic head nod, nearly inclined the phrases to return into alignment. Their eyes could shift with pain, straining no longer to look away too frequently but painstakingly listening, searching out a few glimmer of preference that I may want to by way of hook or by way of crook, in the long run, get via the disastrous transport of a speech. Lastly got here the arrival of sympathy as I ultimately determined the way to struggle to shut out the terrifying talk. During the ones times, I desperately desired to mop up the mess I'd manufactured from my phrases and scurry to my seat, attempting with all my may additionally to grin via sullen eyes, sunken shoulders, and a sulky mood.

While I choice that I actually have to say that that is a fictitious tale, it is, in fact, a actual non-public account. Thanks to a outstanding deal of introspection and formalized strategies, it's miles now a part of my tale that I no longer deny but freely admit as a real lived enjoy and one that such a lot of humans at some point of the globe face in their private manner, in a few unspecified time in the destiny of their private every day stroll of existence. Thankfully I did discover my voice and am now capable of guide others to find out and hook up with their non-public voice.

This ebook is for you and approximately your little one who stutters. This e-book is for adults who stutter and need to be the man or woman you desired on the identical time as you had been greater youthful. This ebook is an educational tool for dad and mom and experts who are organized to vicinity a name for on how stuttering is considered and the manner it affects the people they love.

As a speech-language pathologist, I certainly have the honor of presenting help to you, your children and different families, via customized offerings due to no longer only my specialised education in speech however moreover my studies as nicely. As you dive truly and surely into this e-book, it's far my desire that you see your self or loved one and consequently empower you to better recognize the ache elements and triumphs via the lived critiques of others while reflecting on elements of your very personal tale.

Allow me to percent further on how the tale of others has impacted me each in my opinion and professionally. It is thru these recollections that we're capable of thoroughly observe our hearts and minds in this topic due to the fact the state of affairs of stuttering is not satisfactory a social-emotional adventure however also a tangible one. When we're capable of in fact and unashamedly very very very own our story, we can strategically pass forward in the direction of solutions and techniques of success as it relates to stuttering at the same time as acknowledging the basis problems of speech.

Let me share a story with you approximately a more youthful guy. I will name him Blake. Blake is slight-mannered, inquisitive, and athletic. Blake is a male in his late young adults who obtained a excessive stutter after what become imagined to be a habitual surgical treatment lengthy beyond tremendously incorrect. While his mom changed into involved and hysterical, he arrived at my place of job mildly confused by using way of the modern-day onset of stuttering. Having been fluent in advance than his damage, Blake now exhibited lengthy blocks (pauses) on the begin of each other phrase, which end up determined through using behaviors that might gift as regular to most or a clinical emergency to others. It modified into throughout his first go to that he pondered on his demanding surgical revel in. While he was unable to don't forget all of the sports leading as lots as the onset of his stuttering, he couldn't erase from his mind what he described as a feel of deep scraping and excruciating ache in the direction of his surgical treatment. Subsequently, what determined the surgical treatment modified into excessive stuttering ailment characterized by means of using manner of extended blocks (i.E., pauses), complete phrase repetitions, element phrase repetitions, and ordinary body responses. Demonstrated thru premature eye blinks, hand gestures, and head nods.

At seventeen-years-vintage, this extra younger affected man or woman now self-diagnosed as one among sort of 3 million Americans who stutter. If you're inquisitive, like me, and armed with speedy-fireside questions, you're possibly wondering why and the way this could have befell.

So, in which can we move while we need solutions? Often we can find ourselves scouring the internet to appearance up a few undetermined, impossible, fantastic cause "why' for one detail or each special.

Searching for answers to determine out," Is this ordinary? "Why does my child do that? Or "what takes area whilst you?Google has come to be the gold favored for any and all matters to comprehend or DIY (e.G., "diagnose it yourself").

In fact, the maximum searched or famous key phrases on google range from "weather" within the primary spot to "prodigy" within the fifty-6th spot. Surprisingly the maximum asked question on Google is "what is my IP" likely a great deal much less fantastically the 16th maximum requested question is "the manner to get pregnant" (#fiftygoes to "a way to make love" #ninety one "how many humans are in the worldwide" #ninety nine what is the because of this of existence). Why am I bringing up this at all, and the way is it applicable to you? My point is that we're all in a few way, seeking out answers. We are all in a few manner seeking out to define our motive. In a few way, all people want to revel in a sense of belonging.

As someone who stutters or as a parent of a little one who stutters, belonging, and reputation might be at the very top of your list as you come across ordinary lifestyles and marvel, "Is there all and sundry else inside the global like me." Is there every person that simply receives what it seems like to constantly be involved or maybe fearful of how your terms may be perceived on the same time as you stutter.

I will percentage some information on this book on stuttering, and I will provide terms and theories related to stuttering. It is my reason which you end this ebook feeling knowledgeable and empowered to do a little issue it's miles that you trust you are speculated to do to make a high-quality existence for yourself and on your circle of relatives, with or without stuttering.

Chapter 7: A Boy's Story

It turn out to be Wednesday morning, and I changed into sitting in my second-grade reading beauty. It became time to go during the room, and every scholar had to have a have a look at aloud. I had already long past to the toilet to save you being called on via the same trainer in some unspecified time in the future of the previous social studies elegance.

And I were to the faculty nurse too often already, and it come to be honestly October.

I knew that if I had to take a look at aloud, it supposed that I emerge as going to have to combat inside the direction of lunch again and did now not experience discover it not possible to resist.

Let me provide an reason of, I am a stutterer and feature stuttered thinking about the truth that I become capable to talk. No, there was no longer a unhappy or annoying event. As my grandmother used to mention, "some humans are just made extra precise." As a little one, I did not want to be particular.

Bottom line is, kids can be advise. Back to studying aloud in beauty. The rule within the class became the character studying may additionally need to keep analyzing until they omitted or got here upon a phrase. You received excessive reward from the teacher and recognize from your fellow 2nd graders if you had been capable of look at 2 -3 paragraphs.

I couldn't look at more than 2 phrases in advance than I might also need to stutter. And that is while Billy may want to begin to purposely stutter aloud inside the front of the whole elegance. I however do not recognize why the trainer changed into now not capable of put an give up to it. And a whole lot of the kids might probably laugh too.

A few times whilst it became Billy's flip to observe, he could probable improve his voice and say, "who am I analyzing right now," and then begin to purposefully stutter whilst he have become analyzing.

Once Billy would possibly purposefully tease me, 2nd-grader unwritten guidelines supposed that I had to say to Billy, "I will see you at the playground."

And that meant it become time to fight. I do no longer realise why I ought to say that each time. Billy changed into larger and more potent than me and beat me up maximum of the time. Except for this one time. Billy came charging at me and knocked me over. We began wrestling, and the instructor got here and stopped the fight. On this event, at the same time as the instructor broke us up, Billy had a bloody lip. Billy's lip had gotten caught on my zipper. And all of the children laughed and joked that I had beat Billy up.

To be clean, I did now not combat Billy due to the fact I idea I should beat him. But I knew that if I let Billy bully me unhindered, all of the unique kids may additionally see me as an easy goal.

What is the component of this tale? As a stutterer, our lives are exceptional. Our stutter singles us out.

As a toddler, that can be sad, scary, and unlucky. If parents or the caregiver is supportive and protects the child from the mess that adults create, due to stuttering, then the stutter is a blessing.

It is like what the late poet, Douglass Malloch, writes in his poem "Good Timber Does Not Grow on Ease":

"The tree that in no manner needed to fight for solar, sky, air or slight by no means have become a woodland king, but lived and died a not unusual detail.

Good wooden does no longer increase on ease. The stronger the winds, the more potent the tree, the more the sky the more the duration, the greater the typhoon the more the energy thru sun by using the use of bloodless, via manner of rain and thru snow in tree or man does appropriate wood increase."

Meaning, due to being tested in such a number of social, emotional, cultural, and academic processes because of being a stutterer, you expand greater competencies. You create other survival gadget. For example, an entire lot of stutterers' interest on their math and technological knowledge abilties. And nearly all stutterers' are pressured to increase their essential wondering competencies.

Let me offer an cause of, as a stutterer, every phrase which you communicate comes with the inherent risk of you stuttering. Therefore, the stutterer is always questioning and figuring out how to say matters greater concisely.

A stutterer learns that there are positive terms that they will be more likely to stutter over. Hence you turn out to be very strategic to your use of phrases. All the above creates the capability to suppose succinctly and significantly.

Additionally, the steady having to make multiple choices approximately what to mention and the manner to mention it and which terms to use makes us tired. We experience desire fatigue.

Decision fatigue is the decline of your capability to make fantastic alternatives because of the more than one alternatives that you want to make because of the truth the day goes on.

We make approximately 35,000 alternatives every day. Most of those alternatives are mundane, like what coloration blouse to area on, which in shape to vicinity on, what to consume for breakfast, and so on. But quality 70 of those picks are life-converting or life-changing.

It is my assertion that given the sort of picks that a stutterer has to make about which phrases to apply, no longer use or alternate mid-sentence that we make hundreds extra of alternatives than parents that don't revel in disfluency.

Hence, stutters are even extra liable to desire fatigue.

Let me offer an cause at the back of similarly; our mind is just like a muscle. For instance, at the same time as we bodily exercising our muscle companies in the long run, they come to be tired. And at the equal time as your muscle corporations emerge as fatigued, they do now not function as efficiently. A actual-lifestyles instance would be, marathon runners. Early in the race, their pace is robust, regular, brief, manifestly flowing and reachable. We have all visible photographs of marathon runners.

As the race progresses and towards the cease of the race, the runner's stride isn't always pleasant, inefficient, forceful, graceless, and requires some of strength – unless you are a properly-knowledgeable marathon runner which ninety eight% of the arena isn't always. In short, the marathoner is fatigued and as a end result less inexperienced in his or her stride.

The brain competencies the same way. Early within the day, your mind is refreshed and has masses of energy and a top notch deal of wondering energy. It can maximally machine, synthesize incredible amounts of facts and for that reason make low-value and thoughtful selections.

As the day progresses and as you're making more choices, your thoughts begins offevolved to tire.

The thoughts reports desire fatigue, that is the decline of your capability to make accurate selections as you spend extra time mulling over amazing alternatives in a few unspecified time within the future of the day. The more massive the style of selections each massive and small, the sooner your mind will become tired and hence characteristic a good deal less optimally.

In one of a kind terms, the extra day by day selections you need to make because the day goes on, you turn out to be worse at weighing all the alternatives and make knowledgeable options.

There are a few well-known people who live and act upon the concept of preference fatigue.

1. Former President Obama – Obama states, "You'll see I placed on only gray or blue fits; I'm on the lookout for to pare down alternatives. I don't want to make selections approximately what I'm consuming or wearing. Because I virtually have too many different options to make…" Obama went on to provide an purpose of, "the act of you make a decision erodes your capacity to make later selections." (Baer, 2014)

2. Mark Zuckerberg – echoed that he have to serve 1000000000 people and therefore

does no longer want to waste energy on minor alternatives while there are huge impactful ones he wants to make. Mark wears the same grey t-shirt to trim down the amount of smaller alternatives that he should make. (Baer, 2015)

three. Steve Jobs – wore the same blue jeans and black turtleneck each single day. He additionally favored to restriction the quantity of small choices that he had to make.

In reality, an Israeli observe searching at parole forums confirmed that convicts who seemed in the front of the parole board in advance inside the day have been sixty 5% much more likely to be paroled as compared to people who seemed later inside the day and charged with similar crimes. The have a take a look at reinforced the significance and effect of choice fatigue.

Debra Cassens Weiss of the American Bar Association sums the take a look at up properly… "the check determined that board members were more likely to offer parole on the begin of the day and after breaks for food.

The trouble, researchers said, modified into "desire overload." When confronted with too many choices, humans are more likely to pick the default choice. In the ones instances, the default changed into the denial of parole." Meaning, whilst faced with too many selections' later inside the day after already having made multiple choices earlier in the day, the board did no longer have the power to weigh all of the alternatives. (Weiss, 2011)

There become some other first rate study achieved at the University of Kent. The check hadbusinesses. One institution had to engage with a strenuous computer software program for 90 mins. The certainly one of a type corporation needed to study a mind-independent video for 90 minutes. Then each agencies needed to get on workout motorcycles and pedal until they had been fatigued sufficient to prevent. Each group may additionally need to select out their private resistance degree.

One hundred percentage of the time, the company who changed into no longer mentally worn-out (watched the neutral video) outperformed the mentally tired organisation.

But what end up extra thrilling is, every institution determined on the same resistance stage for the bike ride. What meaning is we aren't very good at understanding while we're cognitively fatigued. Otherwise, the brain-worn-out group could in all likelihood have selected a more herbal resistance. (Baer, 2013)

Do you understand while you are experiencing thoughts fatigue? Do you have were given strategies for preventing mind fatigue? And on the identical time as thoughts fatigue happens, what technique(s) do you have in place that will help you in a few unspecified time in the destiny of the length of fatigue?

One of the appropriate and most not unusual techniques to help with enhancing and staving off selection fatigue is to ensure which you're properly-nourished.

If your bloodstream sugar stages are low and as a result your power is low, then it is more likely that your thoughts stage strength levels will no longer be ok, and you can, therefore, revel in fatigue faster.

What is the element, I could assert that a stutterer memories choice fatigue a good buy in advance within the day as non-stutters? This information hands us with every other records factor on tactics to save you or lower the danger of stuttering.

We all pay attention approximately mindset. I requested several humans what attitude intended. I acquired numerous unique answers for all of us. Many were deep and complicated.

Often the conversations improved to, "can a person's mind-set be changed? For the sake of argument, all our feedback about thoughts-set can be from the attitude that one's mind-set is usually evolving and due to this could be changed and superior.

Back to the definition of mind-set. Albert Einstein once stated, "the whole lot ought to be made as smooth as viable, however no longer much less difficult." The easy and practical definition of "thoughts-set" that we're able to use is "a difficult and speedy of ideals or attitudes about yourself and your competencies." For the sake of this e-book, your attitude consists of the beliefs that you preserve approximately your child or loved one that stutters.

Meaning, in case you assume your toddler's stuttering is a genetic flaw or makes him "less than" and is thus going to keep him over again in lifestyles, then this is the attitude at the manner to be right away and in a roundabout way conveyed to the child who stutters.

How you spot the only which you love who stutters is how the stutterer goes to appearance himself. And it's miles going to steer how the area will see your toddler who stutters too. Now allow's address terms regularly used whilst discussing the situation of stuttering.

Chapter 8: Straight Talk About Stuttering

I sat in my seat at the huge conference captivated with the aid of manner of the speaker's storytelling and candor. Beyond that, I modified into intrigued through his talking sample. It have become acquainted but craftily built.

I listened closely at the cadence and rhythm of his speech and knew immediately what I modified into high quality no individual else within the room knew. After the speaker completed addressing the goal market and left the diploma, I waited inside the line of humans eager to speak with him about what he had shared.

While each person else asked about techniques to raise their enterprise company and services by way of way of the usage of his a achievement framework, I grow to be annoying to study more approximately his speech records and verify what I had suspected from the immediately he started out out speakme. I additionally puzzled if he'd be open to sharing his story on how he managed to deliver one of these stellar speech virtually overlooked via way of the goal marketplace that he because it must be identifies himself as someone with disfluency, specially stuttering.

What is fluency? Fluency is speech that is non-stop, smooth, and no longer effortful. A character with fluent speech speaks without interruptions or commonplace breaks within the drift of their message.

What is everyday disfluency? Disfluency is stuttering that starts offevolved inside the route of a child's intensive language-getting to know years and resolves on its very own once in a while in advance than puberty. It is taken into consideration an normal section of language improvement. Some kids who stutter treatment disfluency with out treatment.

What is stuttering (moreover known as stammering)? Stuttering is considered a fluency illness.

Stuttering is speakme with persevered involuntary repetition of sounds, especially initial consonants. Stuttering might also moreover additionally include detail phrase repetitions (i.E., He w-w-w-needs a cup), one-syllable word repetitions (i.E., No-no-no thank you), prolonged sounds (i.E., mmmmmmmMac is kind), blocks (i.E. [pause] Happy Birthday).

According to the American Speech-Language-Hearing Association, normal disfluency differs from stuttering in that everyday disfluency may be characterized with the aid of manner of multisyllabic (i.E., ambulance, elephant) complete phrase and phrase repetitions (i.E., I need-I want juice please), interjections (i.E., Ahh; Eh) and revisions (i.E., I see-I just like the dog). (1997-2020) Unlike stuttering, the ones abilties are not enormous for physical tension, secondary behaviors, negative reactions, and are absent from family records.

Stuttering, as an alternative, is large for sound or syllable repetitions, prolongations, or blocks. It is not uncommon for stuttering to be followed via bodily tension, secondary behaviors (i.E., foot faucets, tongue clicks, eye blinking, and so on.), terrible reaction, and avoidance of speaking conditions.

Regarding the concern being addressed, circle of relatives statistics is called a danger hassle for stuttering. While research and scholarly publications advocate what we presently called speech-language pathologists concerning the individual and behaviors surrounding fluency and fluency ailment, technological information can nice provide a lot approximately how stuttering manifests from one infant to the subsequent and from number one years to adulthood.

The lens via which one views the world is how they will enjoy the world and the way the area will view them. Hence, the lens a infant views themselves, and their speech is most importantly common with the aid of using the use of their mother and father and their every day caregivers.

Regardless of generation, it's miles the determine who is the expert on their infant. The parent acts due to the fact the number one supply of facts past what a textbook or technology mag must offer. The figure has the most correct account of milestones, successes, strengths, and challenges of the kid. It is the parent who creates the weather and culture for a manner a toddler views themselves. As a discern of a toddler who stutters, you want to have conversations collectively with your toddler who stutters approximately stuttering and their particular speech sample.

Exploring thoughts and feelings in conjunction with your little one approximately their speech makes what might also want to experience similar to the big, terrible monster appear lots a good deal much less frightening.

Offering language or deciding on terminology that wonderful fits how your circle of relatives chooses to talk approximately stuttering can be the motivator for your baby feeling empowered to use his or her voice. As a determine ofmore youthful kids, gathering facts, listening, and supplying steerage is my flow into-to, choice-making bypass. As a Speech-Language Pathologist, I inspire parents to treatment problems with their infant. It is an absolute need to that parents create and pursue possibilities that empowers their little one to sense confident in voicing their personal thoughts and thoughts.

When you, as a figure, allow for interactive feedback collectively along side your little one, you in addition installation trust amongst you and your infant and foster a secure location for that little one. This act positions you as their number one propose and useful resource system.

Chapter 9: What is Stuttering

Now that you have the data, allow's dispel the most common myths about those who stutter.

Myth: People who stutter can prevent in the event that they really want to; they're virtually performing concerned or shy.

Being reserved, introverted, or a good deal plenty much less talkative isn't a purpose of stuttering. In nearly each case that I've encountered, folks that stutter would without problem save you immediate if they may. Stuttering itself does not discriminate primarily based on gender, age, race, or beauty.

Myth: People who stutter are virtually dumb, slow, and less wise than folks who don't stutter.

There isn't always any correlation between stuttering and IQ score or mind. On the alternative, individuals who stutter have a propensity to boast of a fairly advanced vocabulary, mainly because of the capability to find a word spherical a stuttered phrase. Because of the character of stuttering, folks who stutter can rely on a extended lexicon of words at the same time as sharing mind and thoughts. Stuttering isn't connected to cognitive functionality.

A man or woman who stutters is actually as capable as someone who's generally fluent.

Myth: Poor parenting is the cause for that infant's stuttering (so disgrace on you lousy mother).

Bad parenting does now not purpose stuttering. Stuttering isn't always the determine's fault, nor is it the kid's fault. In many instances being the determine of a toddler who stutters makes the figure mainly protective over and touchy to mistreatment.

Myth: Stuttering is "contagious"; if a toddler hears every distinct man or woman stutter, it may motive them to start stuttering.

A man or woman can't seize stuttering from each other person. Several factors are considered to play a characteristic in the onset of stuttering, alongside aspect circle of relatives facts, neuromuscular development, and environmental elements. The root motive of stuttering stays researched.

Myth: Girls stutter simply as a bargain as boys.

Stuttering more commonly affects boys than women. Interventions are in addition powerful, regardless of gender.

Now that we've addressed the misconceptions about stuttering permit's undergo in thoughts the right now speak about stuttering.

Fact: It isn't always uncommon for kids to revel in a duration of developmental stuttering.

The occurrence of stuttering in the route of early developmental tiers is a commonplace incidence, specially as generally growing younger children are acquiring language at a fast charge. The Stuttering Foundation reviews that almost 5 percent of all youngsters go through a length of developmental stuttering that lasts six months or extra. In truth, the bulk of those gets higher with the resource of manner of past due children.

Fact: You are not by myself as people who stutter stay on each a part of the globe.

According to The Stuttering Foundation, more than 70 million people worldwide stutter. In america, an predicted 3 million Americans stutter. Support organizations and corporations, together with the Stuttering and Speech Suite, exist to offer a safe place for humans to talk freely and connect to others on stuttering and speech issues.

Fact: A-list celebrities and famous humans stutter too!

People who stutter locate success in masses of professions and industries. The international internet can provide lists chock full of celebrities who stutter from Elvis Pressley to James Earl Jones. Our former Vice President of the united states, Joe Biden, moreover identifies himself as a person who stutters. Don't allow stuttering to forestall you or your little one from pursuing the motive that you were set to satisfy.

Fact: Help is to be had for individuals who stutter.

Speech-Language Pathologists are professionals expert to offer assessment and remedy for individuals with communication demanding situations.

Fact: Early intervention boasts exceptional effects.

Early intervention services may have an impact on a toddler's developmental trajectory and increase exceptional results for kids, families, and organizations. For early intervention offerings, visit cdc.Gov/FindEI.

Fact: Resources and guide are to be had for folks that stutter.

Organizations and nonprofits exist to offer training and resources for folks who stutter. The reason of this e-book is to encourage desire and help mindset. It is my desire that parents and experts make use of this ebook as a practical useful useful useful resource and assist tool for people and children who stutter.

five

Representation Matters

"...As a toddler I felt dumb in spite of the truth that I have end up one of the smartest in my splendor. There're plenty of issues that youngsters address that stutter." -Johnny Rutledge, NFL veteran

Unfortunately, there may be however a terrific deal of wrong records associated with stuttering. I've had human beings ask if it is contagious. Others have argued that horrific thoughts wiring is the purpose of stuttering. One element that we can uphold is that stuttering isn't always restricted to 1 demographic or magnificence of humans. Well, identified celebrities and terrific figures in records are documented as individuals who stutter. Many quite achieved human beings discover as folks who stutter.

Notably referred to as the voice of Darth Vader in Star Wars, James Earl Jones is one of the most dependable actors inside the industry. His voice is diagnosed as one of the maximum notable in records. In recorded interviews, James Earl Jones describes being silent for the duration of a duration in his existence on the same time as stuttering supplied as a task for him. He moreover mentions that stuttering is apparent for him whilst he feels dissatisfied, pressured, or at the identical time as competing with outside stimuli in desire to tuning to his very private mind and phrases. James Earl Jones credit score rating an English instructor for encouraging him to look at his personal poetry, which he believes contributed to him becoming extra gifted in his speakme functionality. (Stuttering Foundation of America)

Marilyn Monroe, remembered for her breathy voice and sultry on-display display screen presence, has documented feedback on her reviews as someone who stutters. "It's painful" are phrases that Marilyn Monroe used to explain private hardships and her revel in as someone who stutters. (Marilyn Monroe Video

Archives, 2011) The throaty vocal best that she is known for end up in reality a way that Monroe determined after strolling with a speech therapist to address her issues with stuttering. It is stated that Marilyn Monroe modified into regrettably fired from her final movie, "Something's Gotta Give," due to her issue with turning in her strains.

The former vice chairman of america of America, Joe Biden, has brought approximately an accelerated stage of reputation for disfluency as he has openly shared his demanding situations as a person who stutters. Biden critiques that for him, stuttering commenced at age four. Like many individuals who stutter, Biden additionally mentions trouble with declaring his call, making calls frequently through automatic systems, and putting orders as human beings each count on that they may be experiencing a terrible connection or that he's showing a health hassle together with Parkinson's illness. (Brewster, 2020) Joe Biden's political platform has allowed for stuttering to be placed as a social problem in desire to truely an remoted state of affairs.

As an endorse for people who stutter, the more that I connect to those who stutter, the greater emphasis is placed at the notion that illustration topics. People crave connection with a person this is familiar with. People desperately preference to pay attention from someone who gets it. That is why illustration topics. That's why your infant desires to apprehend that they will be valued and essential. People who are valued go immediately to feature rate to others. Your little one who stutters needs a person of their nook to remind them that they count number, regardless of what! Despite the resonance in their phrases with others, certainly being who they have been created to be and going via the world, communicates on your toddler that their voice subjects. While it isn't always their sole obligation to educate others about the science of stuttering, sharing their voice with others serves as a conduit for extended reputation and trade.

Chapter 10: It's its Own Thing

We've taken him to each professional on the town, and no character seems to understand the way to healing this. He has began to hit himself inside the throat and say, "I hate my voice, so I'm gonna beat it up for being terrible." His father stutters and his grandfather stutters, and I in truth don't apprehend what to do at this factor. It pains me to look him so indignant and disappointed while he can't get his phrases out. Sometimes he gets so caught he absolutely shuts down and makes a choice not to speak the least bit. He receives this appearance in his eyes, and he without a doubt appears so defeated by way of using this component that he has the form of difficult time controlling. I want him to revel in on top of things of what's going on to him. I without a doubt need to take the pain away. I'm his mother, I'm intended at the manner to kiss his ouchies away and prevent it from hurting him. This, I actually can not healing or will it away.

As with some factor and for a few people, there can be comfort in categorization and grouping. People usually have a propensity to be tribal in nature. For a few people understanding that their state of affairs is plenty less excessive than that of each other man or woman is comforting. We will be inclined to like to count on that my situation isn't always as horrible as so and so scenario, or we rationalize that a situation is not as a long way lengthy lengthy long gone as it is able to be. When getting news from a medical doctor, for a few humans, clearly setting a call to a tough and fast of symptoms brings remedy. For others understanding how they may be rated on a scale of severity is suitable. Let's find out the only of a type techniques wherein folks who stutter may be classified or categorised. The label this is followed, whether or not or no longer or no longer it is distinction, disorder, or incapacity, is your preference. Whether your infant's stuttering may be very moderate or severe, is based upon in large part on the shape of stuttering and behaviors being exhibited and scientific judgment. Seek a professional professional to offer a right away evaluation of your baby's regular speech and language abilities.

When requested through way of a decide while this "stuttering element" ends, it's far my choice to be smooth and direct on the identical time as acknowledging the immediately reputation of the individual that stutters in consideration of the mind-set of the questioner. My solution is that it's subjective because it truly relies upon on severa elements. Often hobby, utility of strategies, stressors, and factors, every internal and outside, can contribute to the severity of a person's incidences of stuttering on any given day. I clearly have determined that the ones who've completed the finest stage of fulfillment embody, but now not restrained to:

(1) not unusual notable self-concept

(2) supportive environment

(3) connection to community

(four) consistency and dedication to the technique.

Having a first-rate self-concept permits discern and infant to view the sector and their function in it as impactful in choice to terrible. Your infant will make a notable impact in this global, whether or not or not stuttering is completely resolved or will become more easily controlled. The way that you view yourself contributes on your actions and alternatives. Having a great outlook and the use of pleasant self-talk will appreciably decorate how you engage with and reply to others. An traditional top notch outlook may also will let you forgive greater certainly even as errors or shortcomings occur.

A supportive environment is often a effective indicator whilst putting a modern-day method to exercise. Some humans are constructed to persevere no matter what the situations present. In most times, having a supportive surroundings offers someone the choice to keep going, particularly whilst subjects get complex.

Your connection for your community offers you get proper of access to to human beings and offerings that may extensively advantage your toddler who stutters. Knowing the remarkable workplaces to get hold of professional speech treatment or being privy to extracurricular sports if you want to permit your little one to shine is of wonderful advantage on your family. Being associated with a network of people who are invested on your toddler's success is crucial to your toddler's persevered development.

The recovery technique is one this is particular to every affected person and their character desires, whether or not or no longer your infant is receiving services at college or in an place of business setting. While there are confirmed interventions that align with what is taken into consideration great practices, how your toddler responds to treatment services, and what techniques paintings satisfactory for him or her is depending on your toddler and the way they approach services. Committing to speech offerings, or counseling offerings if anxiety is a problem, is not best impacting the kid however the entire circle of relatives.

Consistency towards the encouraged frequency of treatment periods, wearing out recommended techniques, and ongoing conversation with the clinician is important for development and exchange.

As recommended in the bankruptcy on thoughts-set, how a toddler perspectives themselves as a person who stutters is precipitated through way of the strategies and language this is used by those round the kid. Determining a way to view and speak approximately stuttering is a communication that ought to encompass all occasions worried. The character who stutters, mother and father, caregivers, and the education business enterprise ought to all be on board and selling the same targets. Even at a younger age, a little one want to recognise that their voice can be heard in subjects concerning their fashionable conversation and speech. Limiting a infant's potential to recognize what's taking region and the way it's miles going to be addressed opens the door for questions and capability misconceptions. Include the kid as early as viable simply so they recognise that their voice is precious.

For a few mother and father coming near the conversation on how to speak approximately stuttering can be daunting, mainly if the decide continues to be running out their very non-public emotions and ideals approximately stuttering.Connecting with a community of people is important at the same time as navigating conversations on communique abilities and abilties. Here is a listing of agencies and assets precise to the desires of people and households who stutter.

Empowering your toddler to be seen and heard-

1. Organizations

2. Stuttering and Speech Suite

3. American Speech-Language-Hearing Association

four. American Board of Fluency and Fluency Disorders

five. National Stuttering Association

6. International Stuttering Association

7. Stuttering Association for the Young

eight. Friends: The National Association of Young People Who Stutter

9. Stuttering Home Page

10. StutterTalk

Chapter 11: What Do I Do

I preserve asking myself when this stuttering factor goes to give up! My son has been in speech treatment truely his complete lifestyles, and he's handiest seven years vintage. I want someone to inform me that there can be an forestall. I want a person to present me a few want that my son's whole existence is not going to be lengthy-hooked up around the truth that he stutters. I hold considering what his life is going to be like if this keeps. Like if that is in reality how he'll communicate for the relaxation of his existence. I maintain imagining him as a person, with a way, and a own family, and I can't help but wonder how stuttering will affect him. I maintain wondering how it's going to have an impact on my grandkids. I really need to recognize whilst it'll forestall. ~ Parent of a seven-12 months-antique boy

Data indicates that early intervention is a predictor of superb getting to know consequences. While that is proper, stuttering gives with its very personal unique set of worries. As mentioned in a preceding bankruptcy on dispelling myths, it is not uncommon for some kids to experience incidences of stuttering at some point of fast language acquisition tiers taking vicinity in some unspecified time inside the future of early development. In many instances, scientific specialists will inspire households to look in advance to more extended periods of time than crucial to are seeking out specialized help in assessing and addressing communication troubles. While it's miles crucial to preserve a terrific outlook in preference to succumb to a country of panic, logging observations and searching for the assist of a speech-language pathologist to take a better have a look at regions of problem in your infant is proactive in vicinity of reactive. Some dad and mom pick out out to wait due to the fact the speech distinction has no longer been supplied as a mission for the child or family. Indeed, the kid want to be aware that there's a speech difference to use fluency trade strategies.

For some mother and father bringing hobby to a baby's speech difference implies that it's going to motive the kid to have a complex or terrible view in their very own speech. As a speech-language pathologist, I inspire early intervention; but, I recognize that, beliefs and choices remember whilst serving culturally and linguistically severa humans and households. It is in no way my purpose to impose my beliefs or bias, as an possibility provide facts and permit every body to pick out out how they may use the records supplied. What I do endorse is that mother and father look beforehand to changes that might have an effect on the social, emotional, or educational recognition of a infant. If frustration, distress, or hard behaviors are exhibited, then I inspire households to explore reasons as to why the kid may be demonstrating the behavior and propose that families rule out environmental or developmental troubles. The loss of capacity to in reality and concisely talk thoughts and thoughts can be disturbing for any person, youngsters are not exempt.

Chapter 12: A Hope and Help Mindset

As a figure recommend, it's far vital to speak together together along with your infant's teacher to make sure that strategies and issues are taken under attention to great assist your infant inside the look at room however additionally to offer the trainer with perception in your infant as someone. Sample communication among determine and teacher:

Parent: Hello, Mr. Black. I admire you putting in this time to meet with me to speak approximately our daughter, Blythe.

Teacher: Absolutely! We are pleased to have Blythe in our have a look at room. She is that this form of valuable member of the school network.

Parent: Thanks for sharing. While I recognise that faculty has genuinely started out but I favored to take time to fulfill with you right now as you can have found at the identical time as talking with Blythe on the open house that she stutters.

Teacher: I did have a look at that, so I'm happy that we're capable to speak it.

Parent: While it's far important for us as parents to the academics and body of employees that art work with Blythe to understand that she is a infant who stutters, it is also crucial for her to experience cushty with talking up for herself and receiving beneficial resource as desired.

Teacher: I am more than satisfied to help Blythe and similarly train myself on her man or woman dreams. I actually have had a infant who stutters in my beauty earlier than and understand that each infant is remarkable and the manner stuttering impacts every little one is precise.

Parent: Right! We have already started the do business from home with the useful resource of speakme about stuttering and making sure that Blythe is a assured toddler, and it's far our hope that her self assurance continues to boom, mainly concerning her speech.

Teacher: I agree.

Parent: I understand that our conversation has centered on how Blythe's speech, it's also vital which you apprehend Blythe's strengths, pastimes, goals, and areas of growth. I even have provided more records about Blythe inside the shape of an "About Me" picture in your assessment.

Teacher: Thank you for this!

Some human beings put together for the worst but want for the quality. The expression is the glass half of of-full, or half of of of-empty is a proverbial declaration to qualify one's attitude as optimistic or pessimistic. We want loads for our kids, and at the same time as subjects stand up or do not constantly move as deliberate, we have to dig deep to lease a tumbler-1/2-entire attitude. We worry that our infant may be damage. We contemplate what-ifs to try to defend closer to every possible horrible incident. We are mother and father and caregivers, so we want to shield our kids from harm. Sometimes we push too difficult, and we're the ones unknowingly setting our toddler in harm's manner due to the fact we wonder what would possibly have took place if someone had pushed us extra. We query in which we'd be and the manner far along we'd be if we'd sincerely achieve a bit farther or push a hint harder at a given task.

Sometimes we want to characteristic remedy to a scenario and actually do no longer apprehend what to say to restore the harm or repair the boo-boo. No depend range what you are handling collectively together with your infant who stutters or what next step you may be processing to get them to the subsequent stage, remember that you are geared up with the whole thing that you need to be an terrific decide and provide a significant life on your toddler. There might be triumphs and annoying situations as parenting offers many opportunities for teachable moments, every for determine and infant. Maintaining a thoughts-set that is awesome and set on the reality that your infant can be a success is crucial.

It's tough as a discern to have a take a look at your toddler stutter and sincerely war to get terms out. It is even more hard on the identical time as someone annoying conditions your baby's intelligence or skills virtually because of their speech difference. It may be equally tough while someone cuts your little one off mid-sentence or attempts to finish their announcement in reality because of the reality they need to assist them via stuttering, or perhaps they're really impatient together collectively with your baby. It is painful to count on decrease lower lower back to the times on the equal time as you, due to the fact the figure, were tired from the day or worn-out and resorted to correcting your infant or gesturing to guide them to rush thru their stuttering. Although you recognize that you need to allow your infant to complete out their assertion uninterrupted, you certainly could not bear the idea of them getting caught and stumbling over their terms all over again.

You are not on my own. Even parents who stutter admit that speaking with their little one who stutters isn't usually easy even at the same time as you recognize all the right sports. Be affected person with yourself and be affected man or woman collectively together along with your toddler. Keep in thoughts that regardless of how excessive your infant's stuttering will become, it is your process to go to bat for them no matter what. There can be folks that will attempt to mislabel your toddler or restriction their expertise set. It is as a whole lot as you to accumulate their self guarantee so you can boldly face any impediment.

Chapter 13: Advocacy

"People who stutter are quite a resilient bunch...what awesome choice are we able to have? ~Ian Mahler

If I surely have no longer emphasized sufficient, allow me to reiterate that you are your toddler's biggest endorse and primary professional. You realise their cry, every facial functions, gesture, choice, mannerism, and so forth. No one in this global can will can help you understand greater about your toddler than you. While experts and professional practitioners were professional to accomplice with you on choice making, provide research-based facts, and manual tremendous choices, at the forestall of the day, you are the decide. While there are hundreds of books on parenting, on the challenge, within the trenches, parenting is a fantastic instructor. That is why partnership and collaboration at the side of your toddler's trainer are so essential. Teaching the trainer the way to notable help your toddler is vitally important. Providing notion in your little one's instructor on mastering style, hobbies, and triggers will permit the trainer a more described lens as to a way to terrific guide your infant.

Family participants additionally play an essential role in the care and issues that should be discussed concerning your baby. Sometimes family people imply nicely however surely do not have the vital know-how of a way to technique or talk approximately stuttering. Some family contributors can also moreover harbor defective ideals about folks that stutter. Others won't see your little one the manner that you see them. You can be confronted with a few difficult choices as to which circle of relatives individuals you may allow to your toddler's inner circle and which family contributors should be saved at a distance. Your toddler's self-self belief and power are precedence.

Members of the network ought to be covered on your little one's group. Teams might also additionally moreover consist of coaches, circle of relatives friends, kids leaders, and so forth. These community people and all people who are invested on your toddler have to be invested in his or her achievement as it relates to stuttering. Allow network individuals to help your toddler as they technique social reviews far out of your instant acquire. Allowing community participants to assist your infant who stutters permits your infant to assemble keep in mind and bonds crucial to construct their self warranty at the same time as interacting with buddies and uncommon adults.

Chapter 14: Let Your Voice Be Heard

"Everything might be ok ultimately. If it is now not good enough, it's not the surrender." John Lennon

If I go away you with now not some thing else, it's miles my wish that I depart you empowered to fight in your infant's proper to be heard. Be organized to clearly fight. Square up! Be in a characteristic to wreak havoc, if honestly essential, on behalf of your toddler. Your little one desires you in this struggle for his or her voice to be heard. Don't allow fear to choke out your infant's voice as it as fast as did mine. Position yourself as a hedge of safety spherical your little one. You are your little one's fence. You are the defender of all matters superb and first rate for your little one. Parents are to paintings tirelessly to defend and help the innocence and pastimes of their infant. As your infant's advise, it's far important that they

121

understand your feature as parent and protector.

Parents have the right functionality and duty to take care of and guide their kids towards achievement. Success, because it pertains to speakme conditions, does now not recommend that every speaking state of affairs will turn out perfectly. However, achievement can mean that your infant's voice is mentioned and heard. How your little one perspectives his or her voice is supported especially thru the love and care that your baby receives from you as their figure. So as a determine, you have to ask your self how excessive is the bar and who located it there. Is the bar or degree of expectation less steeply-priced, regarding your infant's speech? Is it honest, given the state of affairs, diploma of development, and belongings available? As a parent, you must equip your self with gadget surely so your little one has a whole arsenal of resources to rely on. With you as commander-in-leader, at the facet of your little one's repertoire of approaches, strategies, and solutions, you equip your toddler to win the fight, therefore, getting geared up them for their closing achievement.

Chapter 15: Get Ready for Change

In this economic break you could:

•Learn what this e-book has to provide you and why it's far one-of-a-kind from distinct books about stuttering.

•Get to understand many well-known folks that stutter.

What is stuttering?

Does that sound like a stupid query? Surely absolutely everyone knows what stuttering is.

Random House dictionary defines stuttering as

"to speak in the kind of manner that the rhythm is interrupted by means of way of repetitions, blocks or spasms, or prolongations of sounds or syllables, from time to time observed through contortions of the face and body."

To most people, this definition of stuttering is extra than suitable enough. It's probable what maximum human beings endorse after they communicate or do not forget stuttering.

In this ebook, we are able to show that contrary to popular opinion, the usual definition of stuttering isn't always good enough. We'll show you a current-day, more entire way to think about the difficulty. You'll see how our version shows that there may be extra to stuttering than interrupted speech and "contortions of the face and body."

You might also even examine why such quite a few stuttering remedy plans fail. But for now, proper right here's a hint: maximum treatments fail because they begin with an insufficient, incomplete understanding of what stuttering is.

Our cause is to offer a trendy understanding of stuttering so that you can revolutionize the manner you think about it. You'll boom a deeper knowledge of its reasons and its effects.

And together with this deeper information, you'll learn the way our accelerated model of stuttering offers a clue as to what effective treatment can also moreover entail. Better but, we'll display you procedures you may educate your self an powerful remedy aimed toward the entire stuttering enjoy.

Who Stutters?

The statistics books, no longer to mention the gossip pages of newspapers and grocery store tabloids, are complete of the names of well-known humans who've or who currently stutter: Moses, hero of the Old Testament; Battus who founded the Greek colony at Cyrene in Libya (630 BCE);

the Roman emperor Claudius (forty one-fifty four CE); the Byzantine emperor Michael II the Stutterer (820-829 CE); the French king Louis II (877-879); the English kings Charles I (1629-1649) and George IV (1937-1952); and Britain's top minister Winston Churchill; the truth seeker Aristotle; Charles Darwin; Tiger Woods; Mel Tillis; James Earl Jones; Marilyn Monroe; Prince Albert of Monaco; and enterprise leaders Jack Welch and John Sculley.

A listing of all the famous — and notorious — stutterers in records might be too lengthy for this e-book. We don't know the decision of each person who stutters due to the truth they may be now not all well-known. What we do recognize is that there are numerous people everywhere inside the international who stutter. How many? One estimate shows that approximately 1% of the arena's populace stutters. That's about sixty six million stutterers inside the international! More than three million of them live in the United States.

What to expect

If you're this sort of 66 million those who stutter, then this e-book is for you. We preference it'll additionally hobby your buddies, circle of relatives, teachers, coworkers, employers, and speech therapists.

Here are some of the stuff you'll discover.

In the subsequent bankruptcy, you'll examine conventional remedies for stuttering; you'll find out approximately their strengths and weaknesses, their successes and disasters. Chapter 3 tells how I (G.N.) tried 17 amazing healing techniques to triumph over my stuttering earlier than I finally overcame it with the strategies you'll look at in this ebook. In

Chapter 4, we'll provide you with our prolonged definition of stuttering and provide an motive in the back of how this new definition advantages you in methods you in no way idea viable. If you've ever confused why you stutter, Chapter five offers you the solution. In Chapter 6, you'll study the manner you can use the accelerated definition of stuttering, coupled with a deeper information of its motives, to create a tailored treatment plan for your self that dietary supplements the artwork you do collectively collectively together with your speech therapist, when you have one. In Chapter 7, you'll discover ways to placed your treatment plan to paintings so you get maximum benefit from it. In Chapter eight, you'll find out a brand new way of searching at your self in order to loose you from self-doubt, disgrace, and embarrassment. Chapter 9 will educate you methods to at once manage your speech. Chapter 10 will give a lift to all you've positioned out and look ahead to what you could expect inside the future. Finally, we've added Appendices that provide extra strategies you could use to maintain your head up immoderate and communicate with self perception.

Remember this:

•Most stuttering recuperation approaches fail due to the fact they start with an insufficient, incomplete definition of stuttering.

•Many folks who stutter lead complete and exciting lives and do not permit their stuttering to preserve them once more. You can do it too!

Chapter 16: The Search for a Cure

In this financial disaster you may:

•Discover some of the weird historical strategies in addition to some present day techniques used to deal with stuttering.

•Learn approximately the strengths and weaknesses of modern-day stuttering treatments.

With over 66 million stutterers global, and masses of more in recorded and unrecorded records, it's no marvel that a mess of remedies were tried. A range of the strategies used inside the pre-medical era were pretty weird, and some seem outright barbaric.

As a ways as we apprehend, Moses modified into in no way cured of his stuttering however the Greek orator Demosthenes (383-322 BCE) apparently had some achievement with a treatment suggested via way of the actor Satyrus.

The thespian recommended Demosthenes to talk with pebbles in his mouth, look within the reflect as he talked, and recite poetry even as on foot uphill.

The Byzantine physician and medical writer, Aetius of Amida, whose works date lower again to the sixth century, recommended the number one regarded surgical remedy for stuttering. He believed that surgically setting aside the frenum, a small fold of tissue on the bottom of the tongue, might therapy stuttering.

Thereafter, surgical remedy have turn out to be a well-known method for curing stuttering and remained stylish for numerous centuries. Johann Frederick Dieffenbach (1795-1847) a German health practitioner and H. De Chegoin, in Paris, every devised their very non-public specific surgical strategies to remedy stuttering. But the records show that neither of those gentleman had any real fulfillment with their strategies.

In 1817, J.M.G. Itard recommended that a special gold or ivory fork positioned below the tongue had cured stuttering ininstances. His boasts of success have been quick-lived as evaluations from precise assets discovered that the treatment had now not been eternal.

Charles Canon Kingsley (1819-1875), an orator who stuttered till the age of forty, proposed that a mixture of dumbbell physical activities and setting a piece of cork among the back enamel need to treatment stuttering.

Over the beyond two hundred years, plenty of other remedies have been tried. Most have did not offer commonly splendid consequences. Some of these strategies consist of: direct concept, hypnosis, speech drills, distraction, and rest. Therapies that manipulate the rhythm and timing of speech have moreover been tried.

Some speech therapists have experimented with mechanical techniques to remedy stuttering. The United States Patent Office has approximately seventy prosthetic devices on its test in. These devices are inserted into the mouth or over the Adam's apple so they change the manner you breathe.

Other therapists have taken a "carrot and stick" method. They reward their customers for fluent speech and punish them every time they stutter. Some have even administered an electrical surprise to their customers as a punishment for stuttering.

Other therapists have experimented with a more humane method of remedy: drowning out, or defensive, noises within the room. Others have attempted Delayed Auditory Feedback, a method wherein the stutterer's voice is recorded after which finished once more into his or her ear a few milliseconds later.

Despite their uncommon nature and their inconsistent results, plenty of these techniques are however used nowadays in both their right shape or with mild modifications. The quest to find out a constantly powerful remedy for stuttering will absolute confidence result in more weird techniques being proposed within the destiny.

Fortunately, now not all treatment strategies used in recent times are as bizarre because the "treatments" which have been attempted within the past.

Modern stuttering remedy is practiced thru Speech Language Professionals (SLPs) who are nicely informed with stages that specialize in speech treatment. Their training is large –based absolutely, masking all verbal exchange issues which include articulation problems and fluency problems. SLPs are certified through the dominion wherein they exercising.

Current stuttering therapy, as practiced by means of way of maximum SLPs, specializes in retraining the muscle companies that are applied in generating and regulating breath, the voice- and sound-generating muscle mass (the vocal folds), and the speech-shaping muscle tissue which include the lips and tongue. The two major recovery strategies used in recent times are referred to as fluency shaping and stuttering modification. Some SLPs use one or the opposite; many use integrative treatment options that integrate the two.

Let's take a higher have a examine fluency shaping and stuttering amendment.

Fluency Shaping

Most folks who stutter would love to have surely fluent speech, with out blocks or repetitions. That is the final cause of fluency shaping.

Speech Language Professionals who interest on fluency shaping will train you to grasp first rate motor abilities and/or muscular abilities. These are the competencies which might be required for everyday speech. The intention is to transport your muscle groups in a particular pattern. These styles are known as motive behaviors and are taught in series. Mastering those aim behaviors to obtain truly fluent speech takes a terrific amount of exercise. To make it less complicated with a view to master those capabilities, your SLP will damage them down into a chain of steps.

The first step is to lengthen your speech and to notice how your muscle groups are shifting. Sometimes, you'll have the assist of a laptop to offer you remarks; if a laptop isn't available, you'll collect feedback out of your SLP. The cause is to workout till your muscle organizations waft inside the identical way as a speaker without a stutter. You'll begin through the usage of using making sounds, then syllables, then terms, then easy sentences, and ultimately conversational speech.

Next, you'll discover ways to use "smooth onsets" in that you ensure that your tongue and lips do now not contact each other or the roof of your mouth. Again, you'll regularly have the useful resource of remarks from a pc or your SLP. Once you're capable of without trouble make the sound and preserve it, whilst preserving your mouth, tongue, and lips inside the proper characteristic, you'll progress on to syllables, terms, sentences, and speech.

Finally, whilst you're able to carry out normal verbal exchange, with out the useful resource of a pc or your SLP's steering, you'll practice the use of the ones techniques inside the actual-worldwide, outside your SLP's place of job.

This final step can be difficult and not constantly a success; you can discover it daunting and enjoy beaten with the useful resource of it. If that's the case, you may workout your new capabilities with graduate and undergraduate university university college students, your SLP's secretary and other personnel members, or different places in which you experience stable in advance than taking your capabilities out into the massive huge international.

You also can upload the strategies you'll check on this ebook to boost yourself guarantee so that you're no longer beaten with the aid of the use of anxiety on every occasion you exercise your new talents in public.

Stuttering Modification

If your SLP specializes in stuttering modification, you'll learn how to regulate your speech really so it's miles generally transferring ahead irrespective of the truth that you although stutter. Another reason of stuttering modification is with a view to analyze to speak with minimal abnormality.

Stuttering amendment SLPs are guided through the acronym MIDVAS, which stands for Motivation, Identification, Desensitization, Variation, Approximation and Stabilization.

To encourage you, your SLP will assemble your choice to do the vital workout to fulfill your speech desires.

Next, you and your SLP will discover the obvious and now not-so-apparent property you do at the same time as you stutter.

Having identified what you do whilst you stutter, your SLP will inspire you to get used to the ones behaviors so you're no longerthru them. For instance, you will be advocated to stutter more than you generally do.

Your SLP will have you variety the way you speak. For example, she or he can also have you ever ever repeat phrases which you stumble on in a manner that is imperfect, however special out of your widespread speech. Or you will be requested to prevent speaking halfway thru a word, and to hold onto the stuttering 2d till you're confident you could entire the phrase in a slow, useful, prolonged way.

The final exercise is to exercise speakme the use of the identical posture that a non-stutterer would possibly hire to mention a particular sound or word. You'll be asked to show your speech and may match on "location journeys" at the side of your SLP to reinforce your profits.

Once you've mastered those steps, you'll keep education them to over-take a look at them till they revel in herbal to you and you may use them to your regular day-to-day sports.

Strengths and weaknesses

Whether your SLP makes a speciality of fluency shaping or stuttering exchange, you can probably see him or her multiple times each week. You may additionally even join up in an intensive path lastingto a few weeks for 9 hours in keeping with day. There are many methods that each remedy can be changed and tailored to suit your wishes.

SLPs from the fluency shaping school expect that you stutter due to the reality that's the way you discovered to speak. They don't forget stutter-loose speech due to the fact the excellent a achievement outcome. They received't try to reduce your fears and anxieties approximately stuttering however don't forget they may without a doubt disappear when you talk with out stuttering.

On the alternative hand, SLPs from the stuttering trade college will inspire you to confront your fears via deliberately stuttering and final in situations you discover hard.

Long-time period research suggest that for optimum humans, neither of those treatments outcomes in lasting, stutter-loose speech. However, stutterers who have located to exchange their thoughts-set towards stuttering and triumph over their worry of talking have a higher final outcomes than folks that do no longer adjust their mind-set. As you'll studies in later chapters, we be given as genuine with changing your mind-set in the route of your self, others, and life in elegant will substantially beautify the effectiveness of therapy. In truth, for loads individuals who stutter, a exchange in mind-set is all they need to talk extra fluently.

Mechanical speech aids

Recent advances in generation and miniaturization have delivered about the development of a tool similar to a hearing beneficial useful resource. The tool has a microphone and an earplug. When you speak, the microphone records your speech and plays it yet again to you thru the earplug. The tool delays your speech via manner of fifty to 250 milliseconds and plays it decrease returned at a better or lower pitch.

At the time of writing, there were no lengthy-term, medical studies to decide how nicely those gadgets paintings or on what their impact may be at the mind development of children.

And so the look for a hard and fast up, powerful remedy for stuttering is going on. In the subsequent bankruptcy, you'll observe the manner I (G.N.) attempted 17 amazing treatment plans to triumph over my stuttering in advance than I in the end overcame it with the techniques you'll studies in this ebook.

Remember this:

•Fluency shaping and stuttering alternate are the 2 most commonly used strategies of treating stuttering.

•Long-time period studies suggest that for optimum humans, neither of these remedies results in lasting, stutter-free speech.

•Stutterers who have discovered out to exchange their thoughts-set inside the course of stuttering and triumph over their fear of speaking have a higher final results than people who do not alter their mind-set.

Chapter 17: Hopes and Dreams

In this bankruptcy you can:

•Learn how one of the authors of this e-book tried 17 extremely good remedies in advance than conquering his stuttering.

•Get to apprehend about a scientific, idea-based technique to trade your stuttering-associated thoughts, feelings, and behaviors.

My co-creator (W.R.) has in no way stuttered however I (G.N.) have stuttered to various ranges all through my life.

I have become born in Latvia at a time even as that u . S . A . Turned into impartial. But Latvia's independence become shattered by a Soviet invasion that emerge as soon followed thru a Nazi invasion. My family and I lived in regular worry.

To my data, nobody in my family has ever stuttered, but inside a few months of analyzing to talk, I started out out stuttering. I struggled with my phrases, and as I have come to be greater aware of my struggles, I felt helpless and hopeless. I started out to doubt that I could probably ever be able to talk efficaciously.

By the time I commenced college, my stuttering turned into so extreme that I refused to speak. For instance, on one occasion as soon as I had to go to the rest room, I have become so afraid to talk that I ought to now not enhance my hand and ask for permission to be excused. Instead, I tried to "maintain it in." Much to my chagrin, my valiant attempt to maintain it in failed with embarrassing effects. I can in spite of the reality that don't forget about the small rivulet snaking its manner closer to the the the front of the room in the rows some of the desks.

With the passage of time, I can now appearance yet again on that incident with amusement. I can't say the same approximately any other stuttering incident that happened as soon as I become twelve.

A circle of relatives's dream threatened

World War II had ended. Like many others from Eastern Europe, my circle of relatives and I had been residing in a refugee camp, barely surviving on a subsistence weight-reduction plan: three each day food of "slop". What we could not devour with the unmarried spoon my circle of relatives shared, we ate with our palms. In an environment paying homage to a Charles Dickens novel, there had been no 2nd helpings.

We had one change of outer garb,units of undies and no amusement except communal making a song and football, done with a ball crafted from rags.

Although our schools in the camp had no books, we had exceptional teachers. I modified into taught math thru way of engineers, biology thru medical doctors and nurses, and language via the usage of authors and poets. We each had a small slate tablet to install writing on, even though once in a while we would have paper and pencils or crayons which have been a gift from American church buildings.

Life come to be bleak. However, we have been not ravenous as we were in some unspecified time in the future of our flight from the advancing Russian armies. Our women and ladies have been typically not attacked with the aid of manner of the occupying United States infantrymen. Many of the women and girls who had remained in Latvia below Russian profession had been not so lucky.

The state of affairs in Latvia made returning to our place of origin out of the query. My own family's first-rate want come to be to immigrate to the USA. Because my father end up a medical doctor and my mom a dentist, america authorities become inclined to surely accept us for resettlement, furnished we must skip a sequence of fitness assessments and display that we have been not Nazi sympathizers.

The interview with my father, mother, andolder sisters went properly. My youngest sister, then aged 2, clearly smiled. Then it came my turn. When the immigration officer asked me my call, I had considered taken into consideration one of my silent blocks. After five breaths, I however couldn't get a valid to come out of my mouth.

By that point I had already been uncovered to a few "stuttering treatment". Theor three self-proclaimed stuttering therapists had finished not anything except train me to keep attempting to speak. When I became requested my call, I changed into determined to say "Gunars". But not some element got here out. Nothing! I felt terrified that my secondary stuttering signs and symptoms and non-response may also want to duplicate on my intellectual competence and area my circle of relatives's immigration dream in jeopardy.

My parents instructed the us Consular representative that I stuttered. He want to have understood. He kindly gave me a pencil and a bit of paper to put in writing down my name on. However, in my panic, and likely because of what I'd learned in my stuttering therapy, I modified into decided to say my name. Writing my name need to have been an admission of failure and unworthiness. I persevered, struggling to speak at the same time as showing all sorts of secondary stuttering signs and signs. Yet the ominous silence continued.

Eventually we had been escorted out of the place of job. My father stayed at the back of for some time, and I fled into the woods, hiding out for eight hours. Emerging from my hiding vicinity, I wept and couldn't be consoled. I spent the followingor 3 weeks by myself, blaming myself for letting my family down. I do not don't forget all the information of in recent times, however I keep in thoughts it modified into stressful.

Although college turn out to be in session within the route of these weeks, I had no touch with my university friends or soccer buddies; I ate and slept best sporadically. I can also want to now not speak with my own family. I knew I had swept away their goals — now not simplest due to my stuttering, however because of no longer responding on the equal time as asked to jot down my name. I blamed myself mercilessly and could no longer allow sincerely anybody to console me.

Happily, we had been ultimately cleared for immigration to the usa. I can great assume that the sort US Consulate worker had been uncovered to different folks that stuttered and knew that I have become not going to emerge as as a ward of the nation.

Safely settled within the United States, I started out out the look for a treatment for my suffering, incoherent speech. I attempted seventeen precise remedies. I began every new remedy with a wave of want, notable to have that want dashed and get replaced through disappointment. This revel in taught me that there are at the least seventeen one of a type stuttering remedy alternatives that don't paintings!

Lifelong stuttering

My memories seeking out a remedy for stuttering are ordinary for adults who stutter. Approximately forty% of kids who stutter will triumph over their problem without any professional assist by the time they're seven years antique. Another 40% will conquer the problem with the resource of a professional. The very last 20% will enlarge persistent, lifelong stuttering.

Lifelong stutterers regularly discover that no longer satisfactory do they need to cope with repetitions and blocks of their speech, however in addition they have unstable terrible feelings, distressing mind, and uncommon stuttering-associated behaviors. These lifelong stutterers may additionally talk fluently a number of the time, but in spite of remedy, they're actually as probable to relapse and move lower back to stuttering and all the mind, feelings, and movements that go together with it.

Why is remedy so useless for lifelong stutterers?

We trust the low achievement fee is the forestall quit result of SLPs focusing totally on converting the mechanics of speech. That is, they reputation on what you do collectively in conjunction with your vocal folds, your mouth, your breathing, your lips, your tongue, and so on. Few, if any, remedy plans reputation for your thoughts, your emotions, or your behaviors. Those recovery procedures that do address the ones elements of stuttering do so in an unstructured, half-hearted, or haphazard manner.

People who discover ways to manipulate their tension about stuttering regularly document that they become extra fluent. With or with out additional fluency, an awful lot lots less tension and greater participation in life presents to the overall high-quality of our life. The real tragedy of SLPs not immediately or systematically addressing the fears and anxieties of their customers is that many folks who stutter are lacking out on plenty that existence has to offer.

It's not as terrible as it appears

The first rate records is that there can be a systematic, principle-based technique to alternate your stuttering-related mind, feelings, and behaviors. The method is referred to as Rational Emotive Behavior Therapy (REBT).

The big majority of individuals who discover ways to use Rational Emotive

Behavior Therapy of their lives do now not stutter. They use REBT to overcome depression, anger, shame, and tension — the very same emotions that many individuals who stutter revel in approximately their stuttering. They furthermore use it to alternate some of their behaviors, which embody retaining off speakme to strangers or no longer using for jobs they need — behaviors which is probably very acquainted to many folks that stutter.

Usually, those who use Rational Emotive Behavior Therapy learn how to reap this from a psychologist or from self-help books written with the useful resource of the writer of REBT, Dr. Albert Ellis. Unfortunately, few of the psychologists who train REBT apprehend some aspect about stuttering.

Although some SLPs will educate their customers a way to apply REBT, they usually gain this great in passing and don't make it the primary focus in their treatment.

Why are we so obsessed on REBT?

You'll don't forget that I (G.N.) attempted seventeen wonderful remedy plans to treatment my stuttering — none of which labored. My search for a treatment in the end led me into the place of business of Albert Ellis, the writer of Rational Emotive Behavior Therapy. Dr. Ellis quick convinced me that I have to get hold of myself whether or not or no longer or no longer or not I stuttered; I did not need to speak fluently. Paradoxically, the moment I gave up the need to stop stuttering, I actually have turn out to be a whole lot more fluent. In nearly no time in any respect, Dr. Ellis grow to be able to acquire what seventeen SLPs had did now not do: teach me to talk with imperfect fluency and to enjoy my lifestyles no matter how I communicate!

If REBT can offer existence-changing advantages to folks that stutter, why is it that so few SLPs train their clients to use it? We seemotives for REBT's absence in the remedy of stuttering: (1) SLPs who know masses approximately stuttering don't recognize a good buy about REBT; and (2) psychologists who realise masses approximately REBT don't recognize lots approximately stuttering. As a result, those who stutter and characteristic the associated risky feelings, thoughts, and moves that go with stuttering are missing out at the blessings that an proof-based remedy can supply to them. What is missing from the remedy of stuttering is an method that mixes the outstanding techniques of addressing the mechanical, physical elements of stuttering with a hooked up approach of addressing your stuttering-related thoughts, feelings, and actions.

Given present era and what we recognize — and don't recognize — approximately stuttering, it's no longer going that an man or woman, lifelong stutterer can be cured of stuttering just so she or he continuously speaks fluently, and in no manner once more has the blocks or repetitions of the past.

The next fantastic final results — one this is properly in the geographical regions of opportunity — is to speak fluently, or with minimal disfluency, for prolonged periods of time. This very last consequences would moreover encompass no longer frequently feeling any disgrace, tension, guilt, or specific risky emotions. It would possibly allow those who stutter to experience a miles greater participation in life without keeping off speaking opportunities.

There may not be a foolproof, assured cure for stuttering. But take a 2nd to dream. Think how your life might be one in all a kind in case you did now not stutter. How may you revel in at the same time as speakme to others, both in individual or on the cellphone? Would you revel in extra cushty inside the ones situations than you do while you currently face those conditions?

Imagine talking with out tension! How a lot more fluently do you watched you'll speak in case you no longer felt traumatic on every occasion you opened your mouth? You won't be flawlessly fluent, but nearly sincerely, you'd speak greater fluently than you do currently.

What adjustments may want to you're making if you didn't stutter? Now don't forget making the ones manner of life adjustments, no matter whether or now not or now not or now not you stutter.

When you examine Rational Emotive Behavior Therapy and have a look at it constantly to your existence, you can accumulate the twin benefits of (1) speakme with plenty a lot less, or perhaps no, anxiety; and (2) overcoming the tendency to keep away from life-improving conditions, which include making use of for a better way or speaking to appealing strangers.

Your SLP, if you have one, can also recognize no longer whatever approximately REBT. But by the time you've finished analyzing this e-book, you'll understand enough to begin making the ones profound changes that REBT can convey.

But earlier than we train you a manner to apply REBT, allow's take a more in-depth observe stuttering, what it is, and what motives it.

Remember this:

•Rational Emotive Behavior Therapy (REBT) is a systematic, principle-based approach to trade your stuttering-related thoughts, emotions, and behaviors.

•With REBT you can communicate with little or no tension.

•REBT will assist you conquer the tendency to keep away from life-improving conditions.

Chapter 18: Towards Understanding

In this monetary disaster you may:

•Learn a extra entire definition of stuttering.

•Discover the position of mind, feelings, and actions inside the stuttering enjoy.

What is stuttering?

If you ask any of your pals who do no longer stutter to inform you what they count on stuttering is, they may likely inform you that it manner that you have hassle pronouncing some phrases. They'll let you know approximately repetitions and blocks and they'll even point out that you flow into your head or blink your eyes every time you speak.

To the outside observer, that is what it way to stutter. But for the ones people who stutter, there is lots extra to it than what our pals can see and pay interest.

What your pals cannot see is the way you feel — how you experience in advance than you communicate, the way you sense at the same time as you're talking, and the way you revel in after you've got had been given completed talking.

What they can not see is what you trust you studied — what you think in advance than you talk, what you accept as true with you studied at the same time as you're speakme, and what you consider you studied after you've got completed speakme. Your friends can not see all the making plans you do — making plans which terms to apply and which terms to keep away from. They cannot see all of the conditions you avoid, which includes turning down invitations to activities, no longer utilizing for jobs you need, or ensuring that particular family individuals solution the mobile phone each time it earrings.

Most of your friends in all likelihood don't have any idea that stuttering has many faces and there are numerous factors of lifelong stuttering which have truely no longer something to do with speakme.

For too prolonged, too many SLPs have — like your buddies — centered almost completely at the mechanics of speech at the identical time as no longer paying enough interest to these precise elements of stuttering: your mind, your feelings, and your movements. We don't forget that focusing on and overcoming a lot of the ones brilliant, regularly overlooked, sides of stuttering is the important thing to coping with stuttering and to becoming more fluent.

So permit's take every exclusive take a look at stuttering, and pay special hobby to those one-of-a-kind components. As we've a study the multifaceted nature of lifelong stuttering, it is important to take into account that not all of these factors will practice to you. But quite a few them may be very familiar to you. Those elements of stuttering that do not observe to you will be extensively diagnosed to unique folks that stutter.

Seen and heard

The most apparent a part of stuttering is the handiest your buddies note — you've got had been given trouble saying some terms. Sometimes you repeat the primary letter or first syllable of a word. At different times, you open your mouth to speak but no sounds emerge. Some of those speech issues get up in advance than you even speak. As you recommend what you are about to mention and rehearse it to your thoughts, you are aware about repetitions and blocks.

Your speech, at the same time as it comes out, regularly does no longer have the equal frequency due to the fact the speech of those who do now not stutter. Your voice may be better pitched or lower pitched. You may also additionally talk slower or quicker than individuals who do not stutter. Sometimes you can communicate in a singsong voice or emphasize terms and syllables in every other way from the manner folks that do now not stutter emphasize their words and syllables. Sometimes you may talk in a monotone with out emphasizing any phrases or syllables. You may additionally moreover even speak as even though you have got a foreign accessory.

Another hassle of stuttering for a few human beings, and this is regularly, however no longer constantly, obvious to out of doors observers is unusual frame motion. Many of the people you speak to may not be conscious which you avoid making eye contact with them, however they'll be conscious which you blink your eyes on every occasion you talk. They also can or may not look at which you snap your palms, swing your fingers, or swing your whole frame backward and forward. Some of your listeners will word which you traumatic diverse muscle groups on your face, that your face twitches, and once in a while your head jerks at the same time as you speak. If they will be very observant they will observe you tapping your right or left foot, or in all likelihood every of them. If you have had a few forms of speech remedy, you might have been taught to speak as despite the fact that you're chewing on the equal time a good way to hide the fact which you have trouble saying a few terms. This simultaneous chewing and speaking may also additionally or may not be apparent to your listener.

Fortunately, even when you have body actions, maximum humans are not very observant, and till your body moves are exaggerated, some of the humans you talk to may not be aware them. Even in the occasion that they do word some of the stuff you do whilst you speak, only a few people can be conscious the assets you keep away from doing. People who stutter locate many things to avoid, and opportunities are you are not any particular. Let's take a better take a look at a number of the ones avoidance behaviors that are common to those who stutter.

Perhaps you've got were given got problem with high first-class phrases or letters. You have possibly decided that some sounds are tough and that you may nearly constantly stutter whilst you attempt to say phrases that start with those sounds. To get around this hassle, you may try and avoid those phrases and alternative one of a kind phrases or terms of their place. You'll find out that you count on ahead and plan more than one strategies to avoid those tough sounds, phrases, and letters. Frequently, through fending off those phrases, sounds, and letters, you'll make statements you had no longer speculated to make or reply to questions with in reality beside the factor answers.

Another tactic you operate to avoid saying those hard phrases, sounds, or letters is to insert an introductory phrase that lets in you eliminate announcing the scary sound. This will frequently get you started talking without a block or a stutter. On first rate sports, you desire that even as expressing this introductory word, you'll think of a manner to avoid the difficult phrase. At the very least, the introductory word will give you a chance to brace yourself for the upcoming war. At times, you might not be able to consider an introductory phrase so will insert a unmarried word — e.G., "really," "um," and so on. — or you could cough as even though clearing your throat.

Get me out of right here

Many folks who stutter — which consist of you, likely — now not only avoid phrases, sounds, and letters, but moreover avoid taking component in plenty of lifestyles-enhancing possibilities. Many instances you'll have a few detail to mention but won't say it — inside the have a look at room, at a public assembly, or at social gatherings.

Most human beings, which include folks who do not stutter, have social tension occasionally and avoid talking up in social conditions. But this tendency appears to be exaggerated in folks that stutter. Even when the stakes are excessive, along with if you have the possibility to apply for a better job or to make the acquaintance of an appealing member of the other sex, you sincerely avoid the scenario, keep your mouth close, and miss out on a terrific possibility.

Very often you can avoid taking a management function even if you have the crucial abilties. You'll keep away from jobs that contain an entire lot of public speakme or talking on the smartphone. In brief, you'll keep away from a few element that locations you within the limelight wherein there may be a possibility that people turns into aware about your stuttering and decide you negatively, or as an inferior man or girls. Because, in your very personal mind, you experience ashamed of your stuttering and choose out your self harshly, you expect that others are making the same judgment. And to you, that looks like a destiny worse than lack of life.

On the social scene, you'll turn down invites to sports and withstand becoming a member of groups along with political parties or turning into energetic in your church.

The extra critical the scenario and the greater your desire is to speak to a person, the much more likely you're to experience stressful whilst speaking to that man or woman. This, in turn, reasons you to stutter greater in those situations. To avoid the embarrassment, you select out to keep away from the ones anxiety-developing situations. In unique phrases, the greater you want to talk to a person, or the greater essential the scenario, the much more likely you are to stay silent or to keep away from the state of affairs absolutely. Consequently, you pass over out on endless life-enriching opportunities.

Avoiding those lifestyles-enhancing conditions and no longer taking part in existence to its whole amount is in all likelihood the very quality fee you pay for stuttering. Being in reality alive and fully human approach pursuing a lifestyles this is profitable and thrilled. When you keep away from important situations and influential or appealing people, you lose the possibility to benefit what you need from lifestyles, you compromise for 2nd exceptional, or maybe come to be with the other of what you in truth need.

Feelings

People who stutter — further to individuals who do now not stutter — experience a wide form of emotions.

176

These feelings were beneficial and essential within the early evolution of the human species. Some of our feelings are excessive excellent and happy; they supply that means to the human enjoy. Other emotions are terrible and very unsightly; they rob u . S . A . Green and first-class experience.

As well as being first-class or ugly, feelings can also be healthy or dangerous. For the person that stutters, unhealthy terrible feelings are an nearly regular companion.

You would probable ask, "What's the distinction amongst a healthy and an awful poor emotion?" Healthy terrible feelings (1) are non-intense, (2) they assist us to regulate to an unwanted situation or to alternate it, and (3) they recede as quickly as they are not wished. On the alternative hand, risky terrible feelings (1) have a propensity to be intense, (2) interfere with our adjustment to an unsightly state of affairs or any try and trade it, and (3) they loaf around long after their "use-with the beneficial useful resource of date" has expired. Simply located, terrible awful emotions prevent us from living existence to the fullest within the most fulfilling manner.

What are some of those awful poor feelings?

As we've got already seen, tension — in particular social tension — performs a number one detail in the lifestyles of the individual that stutters. Any time you come into contact with extraordinary human beings and are predicted to talk with them, your tension stage goes up.

Another common emotion is shame. You also can moreover sense ashamed in case you stutter even as speakme, or you could experience ashamed if you avoid speakme to a person an amazing manner to cover the truth that you stutter. You may additionally feel responsible about your stuttering or about maintaining off humans.

Because you avoid many opportunities which might be open to you, your life isn't always as pleasurable as it would otherwise be. When you take a look at your existence to how it may be, you may sense depressed. Dwelling at the fact that existence appears unfair or that you are unwell-prepared to take part in plenty of life results in deep despondency.

At specific times, you could revel in angry — irritated at people who are unwilling or now not capable of certainly accept you and your stuttering, and irritated at the arena because of the fact you stutter. You may additionally even experience angry at yourself, and often flip that anger right into a deep revel in of guilt.

These awful terrible emotions upload to the frustration of no longer speaking as fluently as you would like. In fact, the ones feelings frequently exacerbate your stuttering.

If, like many people who stutter, you've got were given been attempting for years to speak fluently however were not able to do so constantly, particularly in case you've had speech remedy and briefly advanced your fluency, you will now not be on my own in feeling a deep enjoy of helplessness and hopelessness.

The complete image

To effectively define and describe stuttering requires a whole lot more than a focal point on its apparent seen and audible additives. It isn't enough to virtually describe the ones tendencies of stuttering that an outside observer can see and pay hobby. As properly because the blocks and repetitions and important body actions, there are numerous sides of stuttering that stay hidden. And in plenty of instances, folks that stutter, do all that they are capable of to cover the reality that they stutter by way of way of maintaining off humans and conditions. Any definition of stuttering that does not encompass thoughts, emotions, and movements — at the side of hidden movements further to actions which can be designed to cowl up the fact that you stutter — is incomplete.

Having a whole definition of stuttering has particular advantages if you are looking for a way to triumph over stuttering and its way of life-inhibiting consequences.

By being honestly privy to the multi-dimensional nature of stuttering, you could begin strolling on overcoming it from masses of instructions. You aren't confined to improving your control over the biomechanics of speech. By attacking a number of the emotional and behavioral elements of stuttering right now, you could begin to live lifestyles extra honestly whether or now not or no longer you increase your fluency.

Even if you keep to stutter as plenty as you currently do, if you can triumph over your anxiety and disgrace, you could throw your self into lifestyles and all it has to provide. Never over again will you want to avoid situations that encompass speakme. You'll have the potential to participate in public conferences, take a look at for the undertaking you want, ask questions in beauty, and technique participants of the alternative intercourse to invite them out on a date.

As a byproduct of residing with out shame and tension, and specially avoidances, you may find — even though there aren't any ensures — which you turn out to be more fluent. This is in particular so if, like maximum folks who commenced stuttering as a infant, you're able to speak fluently — or at the least greater fluently — whilst no person else is round. If you do now not stutter or are markedly more fluent even as you are on your personal, then the strategies described on this e-book will likely help you to come to be extra fluent in public. Even if there can be no improvement for your fluency, the mind and sports you'll test in future chapters will honestly permit you to have a extra profitable and absolutely happy existence.

Remember this:

•There are many factors of lifelong stuttering that have in reality not anything to do with talking.

•By being in reality aware of the multi-dimensional nature of stuttering, you could start operating on overcoming it from lots of instructions.